D1453669

For Carolyn Sears
with many thanks

Lee Weaver

How to Protect Yourself
Against Cops
in California
and Other Strange Places

Also by F. Lee Bailey

The Defense Never Rests
For the Defense
Cleared for the Approach: In Defense of Flying
Secrets

How to Protect Yourself Against Cops in California and Other Strange Places

*A Guide for Businessmen
and Other Innocent Travelers
to the Hazards in the 50 States
and Washington, D.C.*

F. Lee Bailey

STEIN AND DAY/*Publishers*/New York

First published in 1982
Copyright © 1982 by F. Lee Bailey
All rights reserved
Designed by Louis A. Ditizio
Printed in the United States of America
STEIN AND DAY/ *Publishers*
Scarborough House
Briarcliff Manor, N.Y. 10510

Library of Congress Cataloging in Publication Data

Bailey, F. Lee (Francis Lee), 1933-
  How to protect yourself against cops in California and other strange
places.

    1. Drunk driving—United States—States. I. Title.
KF2231.Z95B34 1982   345.73'0247   82-48516
ISBN 0-8128-2891-7   347.305247

To Judge Maxine Mackler Chesney, her court personnel, and her jury. She is a credit to the bar, the judiciary, and San Francisco.

Acknowledgments

I am indebted, first and foremost, to three men who caused the result in this case: Ted Gunderson of Los Angeles, one of the finest investigators I have ever met; John Albert Johnson of Boston, my lifelong friend and a crack trial lawyer; and Bob Shapiro, also of Los Angeles, my valued friend and a credit to the trial bar. For help in preparing the table of driving laws, I am indebted to Ken Fishman and Tony Cardinale, as I am to my secretary, Edna Adams, who helped with the manuscript (as she does with nearly everything); and to my editor, publisher, and friend, Sol Stein, whose skill and business acumen helped our last two books to become bestsellers.

Prologue

This is a true story of a personal nightmare that began in the early morning hours on the last day of February 1982. For having done no more than pass through a stop sign hidden behind a tree, I was struck by a uniformed police officer, handcuffed so tightly that my wrists turned black and blue, and clapped in jail for several hours, then subjected to the indignity of a strip and cavity search before I was able to post a bond. The charge was driving under the influence, and after what must have been the longest trial for that offense in the history of the United States, I was finally acquitted by a jury. This is, in part, the story of that experience.

But more important, this is something that could happen to you when you travel to other states for vacations or on business—even if you don't drink at all.

I knew very little about the offense of driving an automobile under the influence of alcohol, for although I have been a trial lawyer for 28 years, I had handled only one such case, a simple one. Necessity is not only the mother of invention, but of education as well. I learned a great deal from this unwanted experience, a good part of which I have tried to pass along in these pages. If you read carefully, and think about what you do before you drive and after you are stopped—should it happen, and it easily could—you may be able to avoid a great deal of unpleasantness, embarrassment, and expense. Just believe that these days the risk of a drunk driving charge is very real, and the fact that you drink sensibly, very little, or not at all is no guarantee that you do not run the risk of an arrest for intoxication, especially if you are a stranger in the community.

If the information set forth in this book helps just one innocent motorist avoid the perils and pain of an undeserved charge of driving under the influence of alcohol; or, should a charge be leveled, if it helps him or her to vindication, it will have been worth the effort it took to relive that unhappy experience in these pages.

*How to Protect Yourself
Against Cops
in California
and Other Strange Places*

How to Protect Yourself Against the Cops in California and Other Strange Places

AS I walked off the United Commuter from Los Angeles at San Francisco's International Airport a few minutes after midnight on the final day of February, I scanned the TV screen for flight information on the arrival of United's 165, inbound from Sacramento. It had been due at 12:10 A.M. The board said it was now due to arrive at Gate 80 at 12:50. That meant it was still on the ground in Sacramento, and might be delayed further. I decided not to wait for the plane and the flight attendant, a very special friend, whose car I had borrowed the day before.

She would ride home at no inconvenience with another flight attendant, so I decided to drop the car at her garage in the Cow Hollow section of town. I made a phone call to a client in Los Angeles with a couple of afterthoughts to some advice I had given earlier in the evening, hung up, and walked out of the terminal alongside one of the women who had been serving on my own flight. I retrieved the automobile from the TWA section of the garage where I had left it the day before, and drove north on Highway 101 toward the city.

I left the highway on Franklin Street, heading for Filbert, holding a steady 22 miles per hour to catch the lights. On the downslope

13

of Franklin, I got behind a confused driver who was changing lanes, back and forth, going very slowly. I turned left on Union Street, something I had never done before despite numerous trips along this route, and proceeded west toward Steiner. The traffic was slow because of a white sedan, possibly a Volvo, dawdling along ahead. Directly in front of me was a red-and-white taxi, obviously impatient with the pace of the white sedan: When it drifted toward the center of Union Street to make a left turn up Laguna, the taxi squeezed by on its right and went through the intersection. I followed the taxi.

Within seconds, I heard the BLAAATTT of motorcycle pipes close behind the left side of my car, and squeezed over to the right again. A uniform shot by on my left, astride a police motorcycle, and directed the cabbie to take the next right turn. Then the officer signaled me to follow, and I caught the words "stop sign." I turned as directed, and double-parked as directed behind the taxi on Buchanan Street. I had not been pinched by a traffic officer for many years, and I had not seen any stop sign at the intersection of Laguna Street. (There was one, it turned out, hidden behind a tree.)

The officer propped up his bike behind my car, and sauntered by. He was a tall man, apparently in his early thirties, with an uneven, rolling gait.

"You can wait in your car, sir," he said as he passed. "I'll be with you shortly." I nodded, and he leaned over near the driver's window of the taxi and began to write. Apparently the cabbie had missed the stop sign, and I had followed him through it, so we were both nailed. Ah well, a nuisance, but not enough to ruin one's whole day. Had I been able to hear the officer's tone as he addressed the taxi driver (as later described in testimony), I would have been more concerned.

I stood next to the driver's door of the Mercedes I was driving, smoking a cigarette and inhaling the cool San Francisco night air. Within minutes, the officer walked back toward me. I had my Massachusetts driver's license and the California registration for

14

the car in my hand. He took them, glanced at the registration, and studied the license.

He looked up at me. I thought he had recognized my name from the license, for I have spent so much time in San Francisco that many people think I live there. He said:

"How long have you been here?"

I was uncertain as to what he meant. "Which time?" I replied.

His face and eyes clouded with a look I do not like to remember. "Oh," he said venomously, "a wise guy, huh?" Between his manner and his expression, a deep hostility was evident. I had not the slightest idea why.

He walked to the rear of the car to check the number plate against the registration. As he passed close to me I caught the odor of beer on his breath. I decided to forego arguing about whether I had passed a *visible* stop sign. He looked at me with narrowed eyes.

"Put out that cigarette!" he said. His voice was not pleasant, and I was not pleased.

"Are you giving me an *order?*" I asked, "or telling me it's against the law to smoke on the street in California?"

His response was instantaneous. Like a small child who hits impulsively and in frustration, he brought the inside edge of his right hand down sharply against my left wrist and sent the cigarette spinning to the street.

And that was only the beginning. Within a short time I was in jail, surrounded by unfriendly cops.

The charge was driving while under the influence of drugs or intoxicating liquors. It must happen to people hundreds of thousands of times each year in the fifty-one traffic jurisdictions in America. Drunk driving is, and has been for as long as I can remember, a major problem in the United States. I have no sympathy with those who drive while drunk, for a moving motor vehicle is a highly dangerous instrument, and requires a sober operator to minimize its dangers.

But in reacting to the annual toll of carnage strewn along our highways by drunk drivers, state legislatures during the past two years have been in competition to see who can pass the "toughest" new drunk driving laws. And while the publicity concerning these new laws has centered around the heavier punishments to be imposed, a more important and somewhat insidious phenomenon is in motion: The cops have decided to set some fierce public examples of their new hard line, probably to scare drivers into going easy on the booze. The problem is, as has been true in every culture for thousands of years, when the police decide to make "examples," they also make the rules as to how those examples should be created, and that is something at which most of them have never been very good.

California, like many other states, has enacted recent legislation designed to "tighten the screws" on those who drive when impaired by drugs or alcohol. It became effective in January 1982. The police forces of the state universally applauded this new law; it filled some with hope and a zest for enforcement, and others with a cerebral muscularity and a terrible resolve. This is bad news for the drunken driver, which is fine; but it is also bad news for the innocent motorist who runs afoul of a cop who is convinced that his future lies in arrests, not convictions, and who likes to exercise the power of his office just because it makes him feel good.

I am writing this book for the traveling vacationers and businessmen and women who are condemned, as I have been for 20 years, to operate an automobile beyond the borders of their home state a good part of the time. There is a new atmosphere now, a new electricity in the air of traffic regulation. It is best that you try to understand what it is, how it works, and what kinds of people are at the controls before you get caught up in it.

Even though driving under the influence (where no one is killed or seriously injured) is a minor crime in virtually every state, a conviction for this offense, called a misdemeanor, can have dire consequences for many careers. And the fact is, most people are not very familiar with the "driving under" laws of *their own* states.

Should you for any reason get arrested for this offense, plan to

16

suffer in a very real sense in terms of cost, lost time, and personal and professional embarrassment. This book is an effort to help you avoid that ugly experience *if* you deserve to avoid it.

If, however, you plan to drive while intoxicated, try to get a refund from your bookseller at once, or discount this book to a friend who is more honorably inclined. I have nothing to give you in the way of help; I hope the cops catch you. But if you drive after drinking when *not* llegally impaired, there are a number of things you should know. To explain, I will tell you what happened to me, what I should have done differently, and what you should do if confronted by the same or similar situations.

I defended one drunk driving case in 1965, and one in 1982, the latter by sitting in a chair and watching two excellent lawyers systematically take the prosecution's case apart. In the second case I learned a lot, for winning was necessary for survival.

February 27, 1982, a Saturday, began in a fashion much more laid back than my hectic schedule normally permits. I awoke in the Hyatt Hotel at Los Angeles International Airport in a comfortable mini-suite, courtesy of the group I had come to address at a seminar for chiropractors, doctors, and lawyers. I had only one task confronting me other than the speech—a midafternoon dissertation on the mechanics and dynamics of a trial, with the focus on the role of the expert medical witness—and that was to advise a pretty young client who had just moved to Los Angeles in pursuit of an acting career. She had to lease an apartment and a car, and find a meaningful way to try to crack the Great Wall of Hollywood.

By prearrangement, she arrived at the suite at about 11:00 A.M., and we had breakfast and a Bloody Mary. By noon she was gone, off to pound the pavement in search of an abode; I made a few phone calls to keep abreast of my far-flung practice, then settled back to finish a captivating bestseller called *Triple,* by Ken Follett. At about 1:00 P.M. I put on my suit jacket, and went down to deliver the speech. When it was over, I agreed to come to an early evening cocktail party to meet a number of the seminar students, went back to my room, and plunged into a novel called *Solo* by Jack Higgins.

17

I remained thus immersed (I was again captivated, even though I realized early on that I had already read the book several years ago) until it was time for the scheduled reception.

I arrived at a private room on the top floor, engaged in the usual glad-handing and picture-taking, and had one scotch and soda, which sat on a chair most of the time with the ice melting.

I returned to my room and waited for my client, who was supposed to have met me at the reception for an early dinner. I was booked on a 9:00 P.M. flight to San Francisco for a business meeting the following morning and I did not want to be "late to the gate," so to speak. A little after 7:00 she came puffing to the door, weary from apartment-hunting in the vast community that is Los Angeles. We went directly to Mr. Peppercorn's for dinner, and were seated a little before 7:30.

The restaurant was crowded, and the waitresses were hustling to keep up with the demand. Ours was obviously harried, but polite and efficient. After a bit she served our predinner cocktails, a rum and coke for the lady and a margarita for myself, and took our dinner order. I ordered a bottle of Robert Mondavi Fumé Blanc, and she pointed out the salad bar. We became immersed in her account of what apartments were available, and what the asking prices were, and the time began to slip by.

The bottle of wine proved to be a problem. When our waitress arrived with it I glanced in the direction of the label, nodded, and she uncorked and poured. We both noticed at the same time that what was flowing into the glass was red, not white. She said "Oops," and went scurrying off. Soon she was back with another bottle; this time I read the label, and it was not Robert Mondavi. She scurried off again.

On the third try the waitress produced the correct bottle; however, a test sip proved to have a sour taste to it, and I asked her to have the Captain try it, thinking that perhaps the lemon juice in the

18

margarita had fouled my taste buds. She came back directly with a fresh bottle, and although it was not up to the high standards one expects of a Mondavi, I didn't have the heart to send it back.

I abandoned the remaining half of the margarita, and sipped unenthusiastically at the wine. The clock ticked on and dinner did not come. I spoke to our waitress and mentioned that I had a flight to catch. She had not placed our order, thinking that we had yet to go to the salad bar. She apologized for the mistake, and promised all deliberate speed.

By the time dinner arrived, time was short and we had to wolf it down. As we left the table, I asked my companion if I should leave the remainder of the wine, about a glass and a half, or if she would like to finish it in the room while I packed my things. She said she would, so I carried two glasses with me from the restaurant. I was hardly out the door when the Captain caught up with me; I had signed the check so hastily that I had omitted my room number. I showed him my key, and he corrected the error. Between the game of musical wine bottles and my omission on the check, valuable time had been eroded, and I was slightly agitated. I was later to be most happy that these little incidents had occurred.

When I finally got to my room and started to throw my things together, it was 8:45. I called United, and inquired as to the status of its Flight 165, the plane I was to meet in San Francisco. It was now due in at 12:10 A.M. I changed my reservation to the 11:05 P.M. Commuter, due in San Francisco at 12:08 A.M., and breathed a little more easily. For the next hour and forty-five minutes I chatted with my client about her acting and other "on-screen" experience, and how long she planned to stay in Los Angeles if things didn't break her way, and about what kind of transportation she ought to lease or buy.

A minute or so before 11:00 P.M. I boarded United's Flight 747 (which was, in fact, a Boeing 727) and settled back in the last aisle seat in first class on the left side of the aircraft. The action in the novel *Solo* was hitting a crescendo. I was hoping to finish it before we landed, so I gave it my full attention, reading at a fast clip. Shortly after takeoff the first class attendant, a tall, handsome black man, asked if I would like a drink. I ordered a scotch and soda, and he set it on the armrest next to me. I sipped at it as I read on, stopping only to hand a note to one of the female flight attendants with a request that she deliver it to the Captain; I was trying to learn the current status of Flight 165, so that the owner of the car I had borrowed and I would not miss each other at the terminal. When the answer came back, I was informed that 165 would be docking at Gate 80, but not when that would occur. The flight attendant apologized for the lack of information. I said that it was not important. I have spent many, many hours on United, which is a solid, comfortable, and friendly airline, and I did not wish to bother anyone further by nit-picking.

The male flight attendant offered me a refill, which I declined, indicating my half-empty glass. I finished *Solo* just as the landing gear was lowered and locked on final approach. When my glass was picked up, it was still about a third full.

If this account seems dull and trivial in its detail, it is—or would have been, had it not been for the calamitous events that followed. As it was, every moment I have described was later to assume a critical importance.

When the motorcycle cop slapped my hand, I knew I was in trouble. Policemen who like to hit people are capable of greater things, and his nightstick and pistol began to look ominous. He had an unfriendly look about him.

"I think you've been drinking," he said. "Come over here to the sidewalk; I'm going to give you a field sobriety test." Had I then known this particular cop's background and proclivities, I would have refused, suspecting that he would not give a truthful account of the "test" no matter how well it was performed. As it was, I thought that I could quickly demonstrate complete sobriety, and followed him to the curb.

"Now watch me, and then you do the same thing," he said, doing a heel-to-toe walk along one of the concrete joints in the sidewalk in a manner that I thought was wobbly. I started to follow as asked, when he barked: "Wait! I'm not through showing you how." His anger was mounting. I took about five steps in the prescribed fashion, reversed direction, and retraced those steps. I thought that might end the matter. I had been quite steady despite the slight incline involved and the fact that I was wearing soft leather boots with two-inch heels.

"I'm not satisfied with that," he said.

"You ought to be," I replied. "I was steadier than you were." He was not pleased. I next got a shove in the back. "I may put you under arrest," he said.

"If you do, that would be a false arrest, and you know it." I had a faint hope that he might reflect on what he was doing, but it was not to be. I began to think about that nightstick and pistol, and called to some bystanders on the other side of the street:

"Would you people come over here? This officer is being abusive!" He held up his hand like a traffic officer at an intersection, and they stayed put. But at least he knew he was being watched. He then read to me from a form on his clipboard an instruction I couldn't believe:

"You are now required to take a sobriety test. You may select a chemical breath test, a blood test, or a urine test. *You have no right to the advice of a lawyer before you decide which test to take.* If you refuse to be tested, you will lose your right to operate a motor vehicle for six months."

The United States Supreme Court has said on many occasions and in many ways that the right to counsel is critical, and may not be refused or withheld by law enforcement officers. Indeed, prior to interrogation it is mandatory to advise a citizen that he *does* have an absolute right to confer with a lawyer. If the officer was in fact reading from his printed form and not making this instruction up,

21

it seemed that California had gone berserk in its desire to ensnare motorists suspected of operating under the influence. How could a layman be expected to know the nature of these three tests, or how they should be administered, or what safeguards to insist upon to insure the integrity of the results? I had never tried a drunk-driving case where chemical tests were involved, but I had been told by lawyers of long experience to regard any police-administered test with a jaundiced eye.

I told the officer that based upon my recent experience on the sidewalk, I was not interested in any tests to be administered by him, and asked to speak with his superior. He answered by hand-cuffing my hands behind my back in a painfully tight fashion, and stepping back to his motorcycle radio to call for a squad car to cart me away to the station. I later learned that in the course of this transmission he said: "I've got a famous lawyer here who's after my job," a reference no doubt to the observation I had made about a false arrest.

A police station house is no place to be at 1:00 A.M. on a Sunday morning. When I arrived, I was seated on a wooden bench and cuffed to a rail behind it. My demand to be allowed a phone call to a lawyer went unheeded for a while; then I was told that I would have to be booked first. I was taken to the booking desk, relieved of everything in my pockets and my necktie, and directed to a pay phone three feet away. Under California law the police are required to offer you a phone where you may talk *privately*, without a police audience. This rule, like many others that night, was ignored.

As I was about to dial information to learn the residence number of a friend and colleague named Ted Kleines, with my fingers crossed in the hope that his number was listed, the arresting officer's "superior" showed up. He was a graying veteran of the traffic force named Sergeant McKenzie, who immediately dashed all prospect of any reasonable conversation by saying belligerently, in a wonderful display of professionalism and impartiality: "You're a disgrace to your profession!"

22

Since I was wearing a three-piece dark pinstriped suit, polished black boots, and a white shirt (minus, by now, my necktie) and standing erect on my own two feet, it was apparent that his remark was not triggered by anything he saw or heard. He was leading with his chin, set to protect his protégé, with no interest at all in what had happened. I later learned that Sergeant McKenzie had every reason to expect that his boy had stepped out of line *without* asking any questions, based on past experience.

He demanded in rough tones that I submit to a chemical breath test called the "Breathalyzer" which, it turned out, he himself intended to administer. I replied that I would agree *provided* that a neutral expert be present to guarantee the impartiality of the results. Sergeant McKenzie wanted no part of such an arrangement. He did not tell me that if I selected the blood test it would be administered in a hospital, or that I had the right to a test by an expert of my own choice immediately after the one administered by the police.

With the test issue at a standstill I called Ted Kleines, much to the chagrin of Sergeant McKenzie, who kept repeating his demands while I was trying to talk. I had known Ted since we worked together on the defense of Patty Hearst in 1975 and I was grateful to find him at home. I explained my circumstances to him and described the prohibition against conferring with counsel that Sergeant McKenzie kept insisting upon. Ted—whose practice is civil, although he tried criminal cases years ago—said that such a demand was nonsense, which was comforting since I had already ignored it by calling him. He said that he would dispatch a bondsman as soon as possible. I continued the conversation for a while, for I had come to a terrifying realization: The only witnesses in the station were policemen and their prisoners. The hostility of the police officers was about as subtle as the quills on an angry porcupine, and the credibility of the prisoners was not likely to hold much sway with a jury. I needed a respectable citizen who could at least say that my speech was ordered, coherent, and showed no trace of a slur. The telephone was the only way I could put myself in the presence of such a witness, and Ted Kleines was it.

While I was talking with Ted, the cop who arrested me entered the station. He stood for a minute, about 10 feet away, looking pleased with himself. Then he yelled at me, "Get off the phone, you've had long enough." I ignored him, and asked the desk officer how much bail would be. He said he didn't know (which was bullshit) but thought that it might be about five hundred dollars.

"Fine," I said. "Since you know that I have that much, I would like to post bail right now." He knew that I had the money because the personal effects property inventory he tried to get me to sign was short by *eight* hundred dollars, a discrepancy I made him correct.

"You can't use your own money to post bail," he said (which was also bullshit).

Within a few minutes I was in a cell with two other inmates, having been told that I would be transferred soon from the precinct where I was being held to headquarters. One of these men was lying on the only bench in the cell, stretched out with his feet propped up against a wall. He did not seem to offer too much in the way of a prospective witness. The other was a pleasant surprise. He was sober, articulate, and aghast that I was in the cell with him, charged with being intoxicated.

"Why, you're not drunk at all!" he said. I thanked him for the compliment, and learned that he had been picked up much earlier for drinking beer on a municipal sidewalk. He was charged with public drunkenness, but had been held several hours beyond his release time. When I met him he was about as drunk as a presiding federal judge. Perhaps he *could* make a credible witness. Having been denied access to my pen and notepad, I memorized his name, address, and phone number. For purposes of this book, I will call him John Walters.

I paced back and forth in the cell, trying to stuff my anger into a corner of my head. Whenever one of the cops came back in the cell area, I would ask to make a second phone call to Ted in an effort to learn the status of the bondsman. All requests were refused. I was not told that under California law I had an absolute right to a second phone call, or that Ted *had called me* with the information I was seeking. A little after 3:00 A.M. I was taken out front again and cuffed to the rail behind the wooden bench.

"May I call my lawyer?" I asked.

"That won't be necessary," replied the desk sergeant. "You are being taken down to Bryant Street to be released." With that assurance I abandoned my request, unaware that the desk sergeant was lying through his teeth.

Within a few minutes a young cop named Harold came with an associate to claim me. Once again the handcuffs were ratcheted so tightly that they were painful. I was placed in a cruiser in the back seat, sitting on my hands. My request that the cuffs be loosened was greeted with "Shut up!" (Nice people, these cops.)

The ride to Bryant Street police headquarters was an exercise in rough-riding that would have done credit to Joey Chitwood. Halfway there Harold discovered that he had forgotten something, and wheeled through a parking lot to head back to Northern Station, jumping the curb twice in the process. My hands felt as though they might soon leave my arms.

When we ultimately arrived at headquarters, I was taken to the third floor—to be "released," I thought. Wrong! After the cuffs were removed, I was fingerprinted, then photographed. When I complained that I had been promised release, a burly and surly sergeant from the sheriff's department (which had charge of the jail) said with disdain that it was not to be. Indeed, the next event was a strip search. My protests that I had already been booked and searched at Northern Station excited little sympathy. Officer Harold had a triumphant gleam in his eye as he carefully inspected every cavity, ostensibly in search of a weapon of some kind. He took little notice of the deep blue ridges his handcuff handiwork had left in my wrists.

Finally, when I had dressed, thoroughly disgusted (these security-conscious defenders of public safety did not bother to search my clothing, a far more likely place to hide a weapon than a bodily cavity). I got to call Ted again. He was shocked that I was still in custody, and promised to light a fire under the bondsman. To make that phone call I had to straddle a pool of vomit that had been splayed on the floor under the phone by a previous caller and left there by the keepers of the jail.

The jail people sort of lost interest in me at this point, and I wandered out toward the booking area. The burly sergeant, his attitude softened a bit, allowed as how I could now make the phone call I had been requesting. I thanked him, and asked:

"One thing I don't understand, Sergeant: Why is it that a person cannot use his own cash to post bond?"

"You mean self-bail?" he said. "You can do that."

"How much is the bail on these charges?" I inquired.

"About five hundred dollars," he responded.

"Fine. I have a bondsman en route, but he seems to have gotten lost somewhere along the way. Would you get my property envelope? There's enough money there for bail."

The sergeant went to the rear of the room and began to confer with some of the others who were on duty. I noticed for the first time that the cop who had arrested me was there, speaking intently in low tones to some of the jail personnel. I still did not know his name, for he had refused several times to give it to me.

The sergeant came back in a few minutes. "The bondsman is going to be here in a couple of seconds," he said. "Are you sure that you want to put up the cash?" I said I would wait a little while longer. It was now about four o'clock in the morning, and I had had enough police company for the night. Al Graf, the bondsman, did appear shortly. He signed the necessary forms, and led me to the first floor where I signed a receipt for the automobile, which had been towed to a police garage. It is significant to note, in view

26

of what was to happen later on, that the officers gave the car back to me *knowing that I was going to drive it away!*

I went across the street to the bondsman's office, paid his fee, and asked if he would be good enough to drive the car to its original destination in Cow Hollow, then take a cab back at my expense.

"What for? There's nothing wrong with you. I've been in this business 30 years, and you can certainly drive."

"That was also true three-and-a-half hours ago when I got arrested," I replied. "But these boys are on the pin, and they know it. Just supposing I should get into an accident with a police car, or get pinched for speeding and thrown back in the tank again. Wouldn't that give them a helluva case?"

"Oh," said Graf, "I know these people; they would never do that!"

"Probably not," I sighed, "but I've been trying lawsuits for 28 years, and I've seen stranger things. Do me the favor anyway, if you will." He agreed. I was well aware that at a later time it would be claimed that I asked him to drive the car because I knew that I was impaired. On balance, however, it seemed a good decision. As it happened, that claim was made, and it backfired right in the face of the prosecution.

A little after five o'clock on Sunday morning, phase one of the nightmare was over.

27

LATER on that Sunday morning I attended the business meeting I had come for, which was more bad news—but at least it was bad only in the economic sense. From long experience in criminal cases, I knew what was about to unfold. At some point within the next 24 hours the news media would explode with the police version of the incident, and it would not be flattering. Unless I missed my guess, the arresting officer's report would be published. Then, to my horror, I learned that Johnny Carson had been arrested and charged with the same offense almost 24 hours to the minute before me. That, for no logical reason, was bad for both of us.

America loves maxims, fables, and other truisms. The man on the street catches upon them, and they are repeated with a domino effect. Even though there was no possible relationship between the two arrests, the fact that both of us were publicly known would cause many to say: "With this much smoke, there's gotta be fire!"

That saying, although it had no logical application to the coincidence that Johnny and I were arrested within one day in cities nearly four hundred miles apart, caught on. People began to take it as true. Their reasoning is somewhat as follows: It is most unlikely

29

that two different police officers in two different California cities could arrest Johnny Carson and F. Lee Bailey on two consecutive nights, with both police officers being wrong. Therefore, both police officers must be right! Sure enough, that kind of twisted logic became operative almost at once.

I must digress for a moment. On the Tuesday night following this infamous weekend, Johnny, who must have been agonizing over his own situation in some depth, decided to confront the matter directly with the best weapon he has: humor. After all, he has to appear in public on a daily basis and could hardly duck the issue for very long. At the opening of his show, which I happened to be watching, right after Ed McMahon's "Heeere's JOHNNY!" Carson appeared on stage accompanied by an actor dressed as a police officer. To compound matters a bit, he got off one of the best lines of his career: "The good news is, my lawyer is F. Lee Bailey!" The crowd roared. I chuckled slightly, and groaned loudly.

I have known Johnny Carson for 15 years, and I think the world of him. He is a marvelous entertainer, and his endurance in the voracious world of television speaks for itself. I would have enjoyed his remark more had he not said, a little later on in the show, "I had a little wine with dinner, and, uh . . . *I'll never do that again.*"

"Oh, my God," I thought, "the people watching are going to think he's pleading guilty for both of us! How the hell am I going to pick a jury, none of whose members watches Johnny Carson?" In discussing the remark later with Ed McMahon, also a friend and former Marine pilot, who thought Johnny's line about my being his lawyer was hilarious, I said:

"This is the second funniest thing that's ever been said about me; the first funniest appeared in *Esquire* magazine many years ago in the form of a cartoon, which showed two aging convicts—three-time losers, obviously—chatting in their cell. One is saying to the other:

"F. Lee Bailey? No kidding? My lawyer was Edward Bennett

30

Williams!" (The original of that cartoon hangs on my office wall.)

Sunday is not a good day to begin to mount a defense in a legal case, because people are hard to find. By early afternoon, however, I was beginning to function. I called John Walters, and confirmed the fact that he would be willing to testify about our jail-cell encounter and my absolute sobriety. I located the black flight attendant who had served me one drink on the United Commuter, and he remembered it clearly. I found the female flight attendant who had carried my note to the Captain (and who had walked out of the terminal a few feet from me), and her memory, too, was clear and favorable. She did tell me that her husband was a police officer in a suburb of San Francisco, and that worried me some: Would his department put pressure on him to pressure *her* to water down that favorable testimony? There was no way to tell. I also wrote a letter to Mayor Diane Feinstein describing the conduct of the various cops I had encountered, and expressing the hope that the City might do better in the future.

On Monday I flew to New York on business, and put the matter in the hands of two of the best lawyers practicing in the United States today: Al Johnson, my friend and colleague for more than 30 years in Boston, and Bob Shapiro of Los Angeles. Bob immediately hired Ted Gunderson—a private investigator who had held many top posts in the Federal Bureau of Investigation, including Special Agent in Charge of its Los Angeles office, the second biggest in the country—to gather the information and evidence which would be essential to good trial preparation.

Ted Kleines was good enough to appear for me in court that Monday for arraignment, and, like any good lawyer, suggested to the prosecutor, Larry Murray, that the City take the stop sign violation, drop the driving under the influence charge, and save everyone a lot of expense and grief. Murray's response was typical of a young prosecutor who sees a chance to try a "big" case:

"We will allow Mr. Bailey to plead guilty to driving while

impaired by alcohol, to be placed on probation, to lose his license for 6 months, to go to school for 20 hours of instruction on alcohol abuse, IF he makes a formal apology to the San Francisco Police Department!" Murray knew unquestionably that he was assuring a trial, a decision he may have come to regret. I will never, for so long as I live, understand the decision of the District Attorney of San Francisco to assign this case to Larry Murray. As we learned long before the trial, and as the news media gleefully reported in the middle of it, Larry Murray had been arrested for drunken driving under the most egregious of circumstances (when compared to my own) and had chosen *not* to assert his innocence by defending himself on the merits of his case.

The investigation was exhaustive, and demonstrated, through the witnesses I have described, every event of the six hours preceding my arrest. Indeed, we documented the entire day of February 27. But, as I learned by being forced to defend myself, only six hours count: That is the length of time it takes for one's system (except for chronic alcoholics) to clear out any ingested alcohol.

The trial began on April 5, 1982, in the Municipal Court "In and for the City and County of San Francisco." Larry Murray shocked both the defense and several judges by announcing that it would last "two weeks and possibly more." Between them, Bob Shapiro and Al Johnson had tried hundreds and hundreds of "driving under" cases, and neither could remember a single one which had lasted more than three days. Good lawyers can try most murder cases in less than two weeks. It was apparent that this misdemeanor case had grown into something akin to all-out warfare.

Before jury selection began, there were hearings before the judge, a woman named Maxine Mackler Chesney. She was a former prosecutor, in her late thirties, petite, blonde, vivacious, bright, and—thank heaven—made of the stuff that every trial lawyer and litigant hope to find in the person in charge of a trial. We had barely begun when I called a hurried conference with Bob and Al.

"I like this judge," I said. "I think we ought to waive jury."

Both men nodded. "It will take a lot for an elected official to rule for you and against the City," said Bob, "but we've got the evidence and I think that she's got the courage to call it straight." I looked at Al. We had practiced together for many years; indeed, when I was in law school, I had worked for *him* as an investigator. Neither of us had much use for bench trials unless we were very confident of the strength of the person presiding.

"It's a shot," he said, "but a good shot. And I say that even though I'm told that she used to be Larry Murray's boss. Let's go with it."

We offered to waive jury. Larry Murray said he would have to check with his boss. In California, as in federal courts, you cannot waive a jury without the consent of the prosecution. In many other jurisdictions a defendant has an absolute right to make the selection, which is the better rule. When the government's lawyers are allowed to register a vote of "No confidence" in the government's judges, something is wrong. We knew from the look that had crossed Murray's face when we made the offer that he and his bosses—Arlo Smith, the district attorney, and Donald Jacobson, the first assistant—were going to refuse. We just didn't know how.

We hadn't long to wait. Murray was soon back with his basis for rejecting Judge Chesney as the finder of fact in the case. Should the judge acquit me, he didn't want the public to think that she had been biased in favor of a fellow member of the bar, he explained. That was a sorry piece of bullshit! Why should an assistant district attorney who had told all and sundry that he had a very strong case agonize over the consequences to be suffered by the *trial judge* in the event of an *acquittal?* Trial judges who act conscientiously daily run the risk of public criticism, and the good ones are perfectly capable of living with it. That Murray was feeling uncomfortable about his presentation was evident when he made it, and more evident when he said to Al Johnson in whispered tones: "Make that motion again before the trial starts; I'll try to convince my boss that we ought to go along." Just to call his bluff, we did. He refused again.

Because we were trying a case that the news media had adopted as their own, we had the advantage of a great deal of "call-in" information. People had read about what had happened and about the pending trial, and had spent their own money to call my office in Boston to offer help. A large part of what we got dealt with Peter Canaan, the cop who arrested me. He had a most interesting background. This information was not too surprising. I had noticed, when he was berating me at Northern Station for talking to Ted Kleines too long, that he had a *shark* tatooed on his right forearm. I mean, really, what man wants to present himself to the world as a shark, the most mindless and vicious of all living creatures? (If you haven't seen *Jaws,* do so at once.)

Canaan had a fascinating history. There had been a number of complaints filed against him, including one when his own department had recommended discipline because of the use of excessive force during the arrest of an allegedly intoxicated person. Also, he had abused an Argentinian citizen following an arrest for speeding because his victim had said he would fight the case in court, according to the sworn testimony of that gentleman. The grounds for that arrest? Driving under the influence of alcohol! The Argentinian had submitted to a Breathalyzer test, which was totally negative, and was *still* held in custody for several hours before being released, a favorite police tactic.

What we didn't learn until after the trial ended was that Peter Canaan, 6 days after he arrested me, *fired his pistol* at a 19-year-old Chinese youth who was trying to get away from him following an alleged traffic violation.

Despite all of this, Judge Chesney ruled that Canaan's background could not be used against him. Had he charged me with assault on a police officer (which a cop will often do when he hits a

34

subject, on the notion that the best defense is a good offense) this material would have been admitted against him. Perhaps he was smart enough to know that. We learned that he had had a criminal record as a youngster, which had caused his original application for a position as a police officer to be rejected, but could not use it because of his age at the time.

Selection of the jury went fairly rapidly, considering the nature of the case, and the fact that California generally allows lawyers wide latitude in the *voir dire* examination of prospective jurors. This process had its lighter moments, despite the tension caused by the expected ferocity of the battle that loomed ahead. Indeed, one of the responses of a young female psychiatric social worker floored me, for, candid as it was, I had never heard anything like it in a courtroom:

> Q. Now I suppose that in the course of your day-to-day work you have quite a bit of contact with police officers?
>
> A. Yes, I do.
>
> Q. And has that experience left you with any specific impressions of the police?
>
> A. Sure. Some are okay, and some are assholes.

Larry Murray never objected, nor moved to strike the remark; indeed, he allowed the social worker to remain on the jury, something most prosecutors would not have done.

Another female juror came on with a burst of candor that had the defense camp whirling. When asked if she had seen the Smirnoff Vodka advertisements featuring myself as the spokesman, she said that she had noticed one in a national magazine. It was just about the time she read about my arrest, and thought the whole thing to be hilarious. She also said that she was married to a lawyer, and that while she didn't really *dislike* lawyers, she had noticed that for some reason none of them seemed to be "able to stand the sound of silence." In a more serious vein, she reported that she had a good deal of ambivalence when it came to automobiles and alcohol.

A close relative, she said, was an alcoholic and a constant source of agony to her; on the other hand, she admitted that she often had a drink or two and then drove a car without feeling that she was endangering anyone. She was an attractive redhead whose responses to questions were clear and unhesitating; she gave every indication of being a bright, strong, even dominant juror. Bob and Al wanted her off the jury. They claimed she was volatile and potentially dangerous. For the only time in what was to be a ridiculously long trial, I disagreed with them.

At my urging we took her into the judge's lobby for further questioning, a common practice designed to prevent the answers from one juror, should they be prejudicial to one side or the other, from contaminating the rest of the jurors sitting in the box. She said nothing more that was startling, except that she was a student and had a final exam coming up in two weeks. We all assured her that the case would surely be over by then, and that if it was not, both sides would consent to excuse her.

Bob and Al were still not convinced, and their objections were both professional and sound. They were uncomfortable with the possibility that we were putting all our eggs in one basket. I accepted responsibility for the judgment.

"She is very bright and perceptive," I said, "and will vote her own mind. She will certainly be one of the leaders of the jury, and I do not believe she will be happy with what the police did that night. Furthermore, she will figure out from our evidence that I did not have enough alcohol to *approach* intoxication. It's a gamble, just like a bench trial would have been. We'll take her."

(In the end we had to let her go so that she could take her final exam; however, I talked to her after the verdict had come in, and she was strong for the defense based upon what she had seen and heard in the courtroom.)

The opening statements were unremarkable, except for one part given by Murray. It might have seemed smart at the time but, like so many other things he did in the course of the trial, it was to cause him immeasurable grief later on. Just before he sat down to permit Al Johnson to speak, he said:

"I want to be very clear about one thing. No one is going to say that Mr. Bailey was drunk, not at all. The testimony will show only that he had had more to drink than the law permits for the operation of an automobile, and that as a result his ability to operate his vehicle was impaired."

I have no doubt that Murray was trying to posture my alleged condition in such a way that he would not be slamming head-on against the testimony of the United Airlines personnel, testimony he knew was going to be strong toward sobriety. Murray was using the so-called "expertise" of the police officers to render an opinion of "impairment," such that ordinary observers wouldn't have noticed. Had Murray done his legal homework correctly, he probably wouldn't have tried that particular strategy.

Al's opening statement reflected the voice of long experience in trying cases of this sort. He carefully outlined every detail of my activity from the time I awoke on Saturday morning until the time of my arrest early Sunday morning, including what I had been doing, whom I was with, and what I had had to eat and drink. He would show, he said, that based upon my total consumption of alcohol in every form during the six important hours prior to the moment I was stopped by Canaan, the most I could have had in my system was one-tenth of the allowable limit, a concentration of no significance when it came to the question of impairment. The object of a well-structured opening statement is to leave the jury saying to themselves:

"If this lawyer can prove what he claims he can prove, he will get my vote." When Al had finished, I thought he had accomplished just that.

Murray's first witness was no surprise: Peter Canaan. He

recounted that he had been on patrol that evening from about 7:00 P.M. on, and that he had been sitting on his motorcycle on Laguna Street, just south of the intersection with Union. He had seen the taxi pass through the intersection, then my Mercedes, and had overtaken us and waved us down. After ticketing the taxi, he had come back to where I was standing and looked at my papers. His question, "How long have you been here?", he explained, was asked only so that he could advise me that if my visit exceeded 30 days, I would be required to obtain a California license.

He had not called me a wise guy, he went on, nor had he struck me. He had reached forward and simply "plucked" the cigarette out of my hand. He had detected an odor of alcohol, and had thus decided that a "field sobriety test" was in order. After it had been completed, he said, he thought that I had had difficulty making the turn, and offered me another chance, which I had refused. He had not shoved me in the back. He did recall my calling to bystanders across the street complaining that he was being abusive, but he had never meant to wave them away: He was only waving at them as sort of a greeting. "Hi there," was what he really meant. In Canaan's opinion, based upon (1) an odor of alcohol, (2) bloodshot eyes, and (3) an unsteady turn while walking the line, I was *not* drunk; I *was* sufficiently impaired by alcohol so that I should not have been operating an automobile.

He had *of course* not clamped the handcuffs on my wrists in any but the most normal and comfortable fashion.

When Al began cross-examination, he scored early and unexpectedly. We had produced a series of photographs tracking the path I had made up Union Street that night, and showing that the stop sign at Laguna was almost completely obscured by a tree growing on the sidewalk. Knowing that he was going to have to deal with these photographs, which were already pinned up on the blackboard behind the witness chair, Canaan made a startling concession: Had he realized how badly the stop sign was hidden by the tree, he wouldn't have ticketed either the taxi or myself! It seemed that here we had a real "Mr. Nice Guy," a compassionate police officer.

Before any such notion could take hold, Al quickly established that Canaan hung out at this particular intersection with some frequency, and that he had probably ticketed 20 or so motorists for running that stop sign during the past two or three months. So much for Mr. Nice Guy.

Next Canaan was asked if he had been drinking beer that evening, perhaps with dinner. He didn't *think* so. Probably had a Coke. He did not drink while on duty, he asserted.

The shark on his forearm had been tatooed there years ago when he was in the service, he explained: "It seemed like a good idea at the time." He did concede that when he observed me operating the automobile there was nothing whatever out of the ordinary, and that absent the stop sign he never would have pulled me over. On close questioning, he admitted that he hadn't actually seen me run the stop sign. It was possible that I had stopped and started up again prior to the time he noticed me passing through the intersection.

He admitted telling me to get off the phone when I was talking with Ted Kleines at Northern Station, but only because he thought I had been talking long enough. He was not trying to overhear what was being said or to interfere with my right to counsel.

Al began to bear down. Since Canaan admittedly had never asked me where I had been during the several hours before arrest, and ran the substantial risk that I might have been drinking coffee somewhere with people of unshakable integrity, had he not acted a little precipitously? Canaan explained that as part of police procedure, the matter of sobriety tests is settled first and questions are asked later. He exhibited a form to explain this, and indeed that was the order in which things were set forth. He couldn't ask me questions without giving me a "Miranda" warning, he said, and

39

such a warning would interfere with the demand for chemical sobriety tests, since as to those there is no right to counsel, and under Miranda the right to counsel is paramount.

I doubt that Peter Canaan thought this little syllogism up himself, but I must once again question the wisdom of the scenario no matter who may have created it. While the rationale of such a procedure may seem plausible at first blush, it is anything but sound and can do both California and many motorists a great disservice.

Dragging an apparently orderly and respectable citizen off to jail on the suspicion of intoxication based solely on the judgment of a police officer is a mean practice at best, and a great waste of public and private money. To assert that because of some tangled legal thicket it is necessary to arrest someone and confine him in a cell without even asking where he has been, with whom, and what if anything he has been drinking is senseless. A Miranda warning need not be given to a mere motorist engaged in a minor traffic violation; it is required for interrogations conducted in a custodial setting, when it is known that the person to be interrogated is already a target, and where the need for counsel is obvious.

Once again, California has caused itself serious problems by trying to structure a situation for vehicle offenses in which the suspect is to be cut off from a lawyer. Officers who daily follow the procedure explained by Canaan run the ever-present risk of arresting people who can explain perfectly why they could *not* be intoxicated, based upon their conduct during the preceding six hours, with many credible witnesses present. Travelers who have just arrived by airline are an excellent example of this, for the airlines do not serve people who are drunk or getting close to it. A traveler who could produce a ticket copy (an excellent reason to hold on to these, by the way), would give the officer a lot to think about before he made an arrest based solely on a few hurried observations.

To further highlight the silly nature of this entire exercise, had I not written my letter to Mayor Feinstein the prosecution would probably have come to trial in no way prepared to deal with any of my evidence, for they would not have known where I was coming from or where I had been. Supposing I had come forward and demonstrated that just prior to being arrested I had spent six hours shooting a television special in a studio where there was no liquor, and had 20 witnesses to prove it. What a waste of time for the court and jury! Even if that had been the case, I would still, no doubt, have been confronted by the same cops swearing on their oaths that I was intoxicated. Once a prosecution gets rolling, police and prosecutors are often reluctant to let truth become an obstacle.

The testimony of Peter Canaan ended without any further developments of note. He had not made a *good* impression, I thought, but it certainly was less than disastrous. Many probably expected (from watching too many Hollywood trials, especially Perry Mason's) that Al should have brought Canaan writhing to the floor in an agony of confession, admitting that he had erred, assaulted, and lied, and begging the mercy of the court. But such things don't happen in real trials, and I had not expected such drama here. Without much finesse, Peter Canaan had been untruthful to the court on a number of important points, including the crucial issue. If the jury believed him, and disbelieved me and the other defense witnesses, they would convict.

Next to the batter's box came Sergeant McKenzie. He recalled our first encounter, including the remark about being a "disgrace," but of course quite differently from how I had described it. He had, in fact, asked several times whether I would take a sobriety test with breath, blood, or urine, but never disclosed that the blood test would be administered by hospital personnel, not by a policeman. (When the unskilled take blood samples with a dirty needle, hepatitis can be the result.)

McKenzie admitted that he had not offered me the use of a private phone even though there was one available. He did not tell me that if I should be dissatisfied with the results of a police sobriety test that I could have my own conducted within a reasonable time thereafter. He did have the opinion that my eyes were bloodshot, that I was boisterous and arrogant, and not terribly steady. When Murray fed him the programmed question that each of the police witnesses had been trained to answer, Al Johnson let the hammer fall:

Q. (MURRAY): Now, Sergeant McKenzie, do you have an opinion as to whether or not Mr. Bailey's condition was impaired by alcohol at the time you observed him in Northern Station?

A. I do.

Q. What is your opinion?

JOHNSON: Objection, Your Honor. Not competent.

There ensued a conference at the bench, which was moved to the judge's lobby. Al's point was a good one: Something as subtle as "impairment" is for an expert, one with special training and experience, to pass upon. A layman must be restricted to simply "drunk" or "sober," and no more. When he had made his point, Al had the judge nodding in agreement. "That would appear to be the law," she said.

Murray was beside himself, quite understandably. He very specifically had committed himself to the jury in his opening statement, saying that none of the witnesses for the prosecution could claim that I was drunk. Now here was the judge about to rule, it seemed, that the only thing left that they *could* say was that I had been sober. That would not be terribly helpful to the prosecution's case. Murray tried in vain to argue that Sergeant McKenzie was an expert, but got nowhere. He was left with a difficult dilemma. And then a miraculous thing happened. All of these police officers, starting with Sergeant McKenzie, who must have told Murray before trial that I was *not* drunk, as Murray had just told the jury, now in the face of sudden need "remembered" that I *was* drunk, thus saving the day. In the face of such remarkable testimonial flexibility by these police witnesses, one wonders whatever hap-

42

pened to the laws forbidding perjury. As it turned out, ironically, the only one who did not say I was drunk was Peter Canaan; had he not been committed before the ruling by Judge Chesney, perhaps he could have "flexed" too.

And thus went the prosecution's parade, in fact its whole ball of wax: Between his case-in-chief and his rebuttal, Murray called a total of nine police officers, each of whom (with the exception of the arresting officer, Peter Canaan) testified that in his opinion I was drunk when he observed me. Each parroted the other, and each gave great emphasis to the claim that I had had "bloodshot eyes." This I found to be ironic, for my eyes never get bloodshot, even on the morning after New Year's Eve, except after swimming in an over-chlorinated swimming pool.

Curious, and a strong indication that this testimony was orchestrated and not grounded in reality, was that as we listened to the testimony of one police witness after another, covering a span of over three hours, there was no change whatever in my condition. This, of course, is a scientific impossibility, since alcohol in the system metabolizes at a fairly predictable rate. Indeed, when one is picked up for public drunkenness, it is the policy of the San Francisco Police Department to keep the person in the "tank" for three hours, presumably to become sufficiently sober to release. The sergeant from the sheriff's department who had offered me self-bail, and was the last to see me before the bondsman led me out of the jail, had no good explanation to give for why my Mercedes should have been returned to me, who was, in his opinion, drunk.

I will not belabor the details of the defense case, except to say that to their everlasting credit, and despite some not too subtle encouragement to do otherwise, each of the witnesses I have earlier described told the truth exactly as it happened, and without equivocating or flinching.

The waitress and maitre d' from Mr. Peppercorn's restaurant at the Los Angeles Airport Hyatt Hotel recalled the meal and its aftermath in detail, and were unshaken on cross-examination. All

43

three flight attendants on the United Commuter flight and the Captain, who had watched me exit the aircraft, were of the opinion that I was quite sober; indeed, the Captain had saved the note I had sent him, and Judge Chesney admitted it in evidence so that the jury could see that this was not the handwriting of a drunk. I was especially gratified that Patricia Brask-Herren, the flight attendant whose husband was a police officer, had not been swerved at all in her story, for apparently Murray had tried to influence her. As she was leaving his office with her husband after an extensive interview during which she stuck by her guns, Murray came running after her to say:

"I wouldn't mind if during cross-examination you get mad at me and cry. . . ." When we brought this incident out in her testimony, Murray turned beet red as the jury stared at him. He should have. Tactics of this sort reflect little credit on the Bar.

Murray was burned one more time when he tried to pressure the bondsman, Al Graf, into saying that the reason I wanted him to drive the car that night was because I was in no condition to drive myself. Murray might as well have bitten a tiger. He elicited a very strong response which he did not want; had he prepared his case more thoroughly, he would have known the answer and never have asked the question. Here's what he got:

"No sir, Mr. Bailey was perfectly capable of driving. I would never help anyone who was intoxicated to get his car out of a garage: My brother was *killed* by a drunk driver!" This opinion left a very interesting contrast with the testimony of Sergeant Burly, who had sworn on his oath that at the same time the bondsman said I was sober, he thought I was drunk.

We did have two pieces of evidence, which trial lawyers call "zingers," that got the jury's attention. The first was the testimony of a lawyer named Ira Jacobowitz from Oakland. When a law student, he had worked as a bartender at a San Francisco bar and restaurant called "The Iron Horse," and one of his chronic customers was Peter Canaan. Brother Canaan used to make a practice of drinking in uniform and on duty, Jacobowitz recounted, when he was tending bar, and that they had had some discussions about Canaan's lack of professionalism. He *also* recalled that one evening Canaan was sitting at the bar when he received a call from headquarters on his walkie-talkie police radio. He acknowledged the call, and said cheerfully: "I'll be back in a little while; I have to go beat up some niggers!" Judge Chesney, after hearing this described by Jacobowitz under oath in her chambers, thought the racist remark would be inflammatory and kept it from the jury; however, Canaan never returned to the stand to deny a word that Jacobowitz had said.

Our second jolter was a scientific expert named Richard Kiszka who had catalogued every ounce of alcohol I had ingested on February 27, and estimated that at the time of my arrest I should have been carrying a level of .01, which is insignificant for impairment purposes. To bolster this, we had conducted a videotaped experiment duplicating every drink, in its proper time frame, that I had consumed within six hours of arrest. The highest level was .055, at dinnertime. At the arrest point the reading on Kiszka's Intoxylizer was .011, or just one percent over his estimate. I have no doubt that in the jury's mind, Kiszka was an impressive and credible witness.

My own testimony, although it was extensively covered by the media, was essentially merely corroborative of what other witnesses had already said. Murray's cross-examination was, at best, uneventful.

Judge Chesney's charge was balanced and right down the middle, as we had thought it would be. It ended late in the day, and I had some hope that the jury might choose to deliberate that evening and make short work of the case—there was a federal judge sitting in Las Cruces, New Mexico, waiting for me to start an involved jury trial—but they decided to wait until the following day. After what turned out to be a lengthy discussion and a detailed examination of the many exhibits that had been received in evidence, the jury returned a verdict late that afternoon, nearly three weeks after we had begun: not guilty of driving while impaired by alcohol; guilty of running the stop sign. This would have been a grand result, and was, to the credit of both lawyers and a fine investigator, except that the case should never have come to trial in the first place.

HAD this been an isolated incident, or a fluke, it might make good after-dinner conversation, but hardly a book. I am convinced, however, that it was not isolated at all, and that travelers need to have a new awareness of the likelihood and perils of being arrested for driving under the influence of liquor. I probably travel as much as anyone in America, and in state after state I have been seeing newspaper articles describing "tough" new drunk-driving laws. The mere passage of such a law is a signal to police to "crack down" and demonstrate the efficacy of this new law enforcement weapon. Any time there is a mandate to "crack down," express or implied, one can expect a demonstrable quantum of zeal on the part of the "crackers," the personnel of law enforcement. And while the end result will be a benefit if people eventually become convinced that they ought not to drive after drinking more than a modest amount of alcohol, there will nonetheless be some innocent people along the way who will pay a price they do not deserve. One of them could be you, unless you learn to protect yourself.

The best protection, if there is any likelihood that you will be driving an automobile while in other cities, is to have the name of a lawyer competent in criminal law in each place that you visit. That may seem like a colossal annoyance, and I realize the risk is run that I will be accused of trying to drum up further business for my profession, but there is really no substitute.

First, only a lawyer will know local police practice, and how best to deal with it. Second, a lawyer has access to a jail when others will not be permitted to see you, and it is critically important to have a witness who is neither an inmate nor a police officer to observe you and talk to you before too much time goes by. Third, in case your witnesses—those who can testify as to your conduct, alcohol ingestion, and apparent sobriety during the preceding six hours—are transients whom you don't know personally, someone needs to find them and interview them before they disappear. That is a lawyer's work. Fourth, what you need to do most when you are in jail is to get out. Arranging your release is something a lawyer can best do. When you locate or learn of one in a city where you are apt to drive, be sure to get his home number, for the odds are that if you should get picked up it will be at night.

There are very few people who drink and are licensed drivers who have not operated an automobile after consuming alcohol, and they will continue to do so. This is not illegal, provided that (1) you are in fact sober and in good control of your senses and motor coordination, and (2) your alcohol level does not exceed the allowable limit, which in most states is .10. (The limits for each state are set forth in Table of State Drunk Driving Laws, p. 69.)

It is important to realize how intoxication occurs. Basically, one needs to understand that it is not the *amount* of alcohol one consumes, but the *rate* at which it is ingested for a given body weight. This is because the body rids itself of alcohol at a given rate. If the rate of ingestion is not allowed to exceed that metabolism by a substantial margin, the total accumulation in the system will not result in impairment.

Alcohol consumption at a given rate and *intoxication*, however, do not necessarily track. Intoxication occurs when the symptoms

48

of alcohol ingestion begin to manifest in a way that substantially alters human conduct. Internally, the mind undergoes a change and may be stimulated to feel happy, or mean, or uninhibited. Externally, motor functions begin to deteriorate. Given a certain blood-alcohol level, when these changes in conduct take place varies from one individual to the next, and the variance is a product of *tolerance,* or the percentage of alcohol one is able to hold without apparent internal or external effect.

There are many fictions floating around in our culture concerning the ingestion of alcohol. We are apt to hear a heavy drinker described as one who has a "hollow leg," indicating that he or she has an unusual capacity for liquor. This may *appear* to be the case because some people do not show the *symptoms* of intoxication after a few drinks, yet their companions may be buzzing. Do not take comfort in this ability if you fancy that you have it. The chemical tests available will measure the percentage of alcohol in your system no matter how well you may hold it. Remember, you can be convicted by *either* your performance during a field sobriety test *or* the results of a chemical test; and in many states, if you exceed the limits of the chemical test you *will* be convicted by law unless the jury is persuaded that the test was improperly conducted. In some states the chemical test results are merely *presumptive* evidence: They can be overcome by evidence of your ability to function normally, but for purposes of operating a motor vehicle, the trend is decidedly toward a *conclusive,* or unrebuttable, presumption of intoxication.

You may believe that what you eat with what you drink will protect your state of sobriety, and that belief may be pegged to experience. People often explain that they got "bombed" because they went to a cocktail party on an empty stomach. They in fact got intoxicated because of the *rate* at which alcohol was poured into the stomach, absorbed by the blood stream, and then by the brain. The amount ingested is not relevant except against a time frame, because of the metabolic factor of the human system.

An ounce of liquor—rum, vodka, tequila, gin, scotch, bourbon,

49

or rye—will be 43-50 percent alcohol, and for purposes of these guidelines is a "drink." Most wine contains 11-13 percent alcohol, and thus a four-ounce glass of wine is also a "drink." As for liquor, these figures refer to that served in the United States; in Great Britain, for instance, the same brand names will have a lower alcohol content, which may induce you to drink more than you normally would. Take no comfort in this diminished alcohol percentage, however; intoxication merely sneaks up on you more insidiously.

An average adult can absorb one "drink" per hour without registering noticeably on a chemical test, because that is the normal rate at which one "burns off" alcohol, and we are interested only in alcohol and its rate of ingestion. You may make yourself *feel* lousy by the way you mix your elixirs, but the scientific tests ignore all that; they measure only the amount of alcohol in your system at the time the test is given.

No matter what you drink, if you have too many drinks in an hour, you will be intoxicated for about 20 to 30 minutes past your "peak." The peak may be thought of as the point at which the rate of ingestion is at its greatest versus the rate of release, or "burn off." When this occurs, there is only one remedy: WAIT! Time will get rid of the alcohol and the fuzziness in your motor system, and nothing else will, period.

You can drink all the black coffee you want, and it may make you feel more alert because of the stimulus of the caffeine. It may also make you feel more able to take the responsibility for handling the controls of an automobile. It will not, however, noticeably improve your ability to pass a chemical test for alcohol in the system.

A glass or two of milk before the cocktail party may make you feel better, especially if you're convinced that it will, but it won't change the amount of alcohol that remains in your system once you ingest it. Only time will do that. It may indeed slow your rate of alcohol absorption, as a meal will, and thus you will not feel "hit" so quickly. You may not feel intoxicated, or act as if you are, but nevertheless the chemical test will show what's in your system. Therefore, if you decide (and you should decide) to avoid the perils of a zealous police attitude, you must keep track of two things:

1. How much alcohol you have consumed during the six hours prior to your wish to drive somewhere, and at what intervals those drinks were consumed; and,
2. How much "burn off" time has gone by since you had the last one, or several, as the case may be. Your system should get rid of about one drink an hour.

The overt symptoms of intoxication, from a slight "buzz" to unconsciousness, are well known to most of us. Ordinarily there will be an odor of alcohol about the breath; this can be terribly strong in one who is quite sober. Depending on the body's tolerance for liquor (and here people vary considerably) there may be a dilation of the pupils of the eyes as well as a watery appearance; after a long drinking bout, the eyes may appear to be bloodshot. The skin may be flushed, the speech slurred, and the gait unsteady. If you find any of these symptoms afflicting you, sit tight for a while. You are not fit to drive, and any police officer who encounters you is going to build a strong case with or without a chemical test. These symptoms are classic, and are likely to be persuasive to almost any jury.

Field sobriety tests vary, but most include the following:

1. Walking a straight line, heel to toe, with a reverse in direction after about five steps. This is an unnatural way to walk at best, even more so if the shoe has a raised heel, and much more difficult than you might think if the surface being used is an incline, even though slight.
2. Standing erect, touch the index finger of each hand to your nose; then try it again with your eyes closed.

3. Standing erect, place your arms at your sides, close your eyes, and tilt your head back. This is a somewhat risky test, for if you are seriously intoxicated you could fall backwards and crack your skull.
4. Stand on one leg without losing your balance or hopping around. If you are asked to do this while your eyes are closed, you are being sandbagged: Many people can't accomplish this feat cold sober, and a fair police officer won't ask you to try.

Bearing in mind that you can be convicted of driving while illegally impaired by alcohol on the basis of *either* your overt symptoms of intoxication *or* a high reading on a chemical test, make sure you're safe on both counts before getting behind the wheel. If you are an experienced tippler, you may act quite normal while carrying a blood-alcohol level that is going to get you convicted even if you are represented by Merlin the Magician. If your tolerance is low, you may act intoxicated with a level as low as .04 or .05. Most people can feel changes at the .05 level, and if they can retain enough objectivity (which the alcohol itself tends to muddle) they will know that they need to stop the drinking and wait for half an hour.

As the table in Appendix B shows, almost every state uses .10 as the critical measure. Some say that you are *presumed* intoxicated at that point, a presumption that you can contradict with evidence of sober conduct, and others say that you are intoxicated, period, for purposes of operating an automobile. If you register .10, you are in trouble. On the other hand, it takes a pretty good rate of alcohol ingestion to reach that point, and if you pay any attention at all to what you drink, you should have some fair and objective indications that you are getting near the limit.

In a few states, the number is lower insofar as legal intoxication is concerned. In Indiana, for example, a reading on a chemical test of .05 to .10 will be admitted into evidence, and the jury will be told that this result is "relevant" to the question of your sobriety. This simply means that jurors are to consider the test results together with other evidence presented.

At the .07 level, Michigan says you are *presumed* to be intoxicated, and New York says, for purposes of driving, that there is *prima facie* evidence of intoxication. At .08, Utah says that you are presumed to be impaired, and Maryland says that you are *prima facie* over the limit. Legally there is a subtle difference between "presumed" and "prima facie," but suffice it to say that either is sufficient to support a conviction *without* any other evidence, or *despite* any other evidence.

As with any "crackdown" campaign such as the one now in progress virtually across the nation on driving under the influence of alcohol (or any drug that impairs the motor system), the sweep of the net is bound to catch some innocent people along with the guilty. There are some things you can do to help yourself if you see things headed the wrong way in an encounter with a law enforcement officer.

First, it is important to understand a little bit about police people. They tend to be "different" in some respects, both because of the personalities that led them to choose police work and the exposure they have had to the miserable side of humanity while on duty. They like uniforms, guns, and wielding authority. Like most of us, they want to be respected.

Police people are generally antagonistic to flashy cars, swaggering motorcycles, and people who come off as "big shots." Mentioning that you know the mayor or the chief is generally unwise. Most times, this is taken as a "put down" to the officer, and it may well be that he doesn't care at all for either the mayor or the chief—running in one of their friends would be just dandy.

If you are stopped by a traffic cop, or encounter one because of an accident in which you have become involved, the *first* impression of your condition will be critical. The cop probably will be looking for any evidence of alcohol right from the outset; and if the encounter takes place at night, you can be *sure* that he will. Expect him to get close enough to smell your breath; if there is an odor of alcohol, the scrutiny will intensify. You may be very sober and still emit a strong alcoholic breath. (Actually, alcohol by itself has no odor, but the other chemicals in liquor, beer, or wine do, and this is what is detected.) I am told that eating peanuts will diminish this odor, but I cannot vouch for the theory from any personal experience.

The cop will then listen with a tuned ear to your speech, while watching your eyes and movements. If he thinks there are symptoms present, you can expect a demand for a field sobriety test then and there; indeed, for many cops the "alcoholic" odor on the breath is enough to have you "walk the line." Any performance in the field sobriety tests which is less than stellar will inevitably lead to a demand (or request, depending on the statute involved) for a chemical test, and you will be confronted with a nasty dilemma.

If you refuse the test, arrest is inevitable in most states, and in a great many your refusal may be shown in court as evidence that you *knew* that the results would be unfavorable. If on the other hand you agree to a test, you are at the mercy of the person administering whatever test is used. Since in most cases the person conducting the tests will be a blood brother of the arresting officer, whose judgment will either be vindicated or contradicted by the results, and since virtually all of these tests can be manipulated by the unscrupulous, you have good cause for concern.

If you are convinced that your blood-alcohol level is less than that allowed by the jurisdiction in question, you may wish to submit to a test that is *both correctly and honestly administered.* If you pass, chances are that you will save yourself substantial expense, loss of time, and personal and professional embarrassment. Because of the fallibility of any of these tests (as shown in Appendix A), this is a delicate decision and one that must be weighed carefully, for an adverse result, if published, will convince the public that you are guilty long before a trial takes place. It will also prove to be a difficult piece of evidence when trial does take place.

In a few states, such as California, you may be told by the officer that ". . . you have no right to the advice of a lawyer before you decide to take a test, or which test to take. . . ." Notice that this is not to say that you are *prohibited* from speaking to a lawyer, although this is almost surely what the officer would like to imply. I personally have strong doubts about the constitutional validity of these admonitions, and will continue to reject them unless and until the United States Supreme Court says squarely that these instructions are permissible. Since that has not happened, assume that you *do* have the right to consult a lawyer, and insist upon it *without* refusing to be tested until that consultation is completed. Always bear in mind that when you are suspected of a criminal offense, almost *anything* you say to *anyone* will be admissible in evidence against you; and do not take comfort in the layman's notion that ". . . it's only his word against mine. . . ." There are many people in prison today solely because of the uncorroborated testimony of someone less credible than a police officer.

On the other hand, nothing that your lawyer tells the police will be used against you in court in any but the most extraordinary circumstances; it is therefore best to speak through him or her. If you have witnesses to cover the six-hour period prior to your apprehension who will be able to establish that you had very little to drink, it is a good idea to bring this to the attention of the police, preferably through counsel. If you should decide to bluff, however, and make up ficticious "witnesses," you run the strong risk that evidence of your mendacity will be used against you, and heavily, at trial.

Although you should be guided, of course, by any legal advice you receive, if for some reason you simply cannot contact a lawyer there are a couple of thumb rules that should be observed. First, I personally would recommend that you consider only a blood test (as opposed to urine or breath) if you are given the choice: In many jurisdictions the choice is yours, but in some it is not (see Appendix B). In virtually every jurisdiction, however, you have an absolute right to a supplemental test of your own election *after* you have submitted to one controlled by the police.

Be sure to demand that the blood sample be taken by someone with medical credentials—a doctor, nurse, intern, or paramedic—who has sterile equipment and knows how to use it. Be very sure that *no alcohol* is used to wipe the skin at the site where the needle is to be injected; there are other antiseptics available. (A solution of betadine, provadone and iodine is one of these.) If you have your choice, ask to be taken to a teaching hospital that has a capability to test the alcohol content of your blood through gas chromatography. If you must submit to a police-supervised test first, let the officers know that if the results are adverse you are going to demand your own test (usually at your own expense) immediately thereafter. This may help to cause the police test to be run more carefully and conscientiously.

When you do have a blood sample drawn, ask that it be analyzed at once. Blood can decompose in the test tube and in the process create *alcohol* of its own! Many hospitals will tell you that the laboratories are functional only during normal working hours, not at night, when you are most likely to be there, and that no immediate test is possible. Under such circumstances there is little you can do except to ask that your request be noted on the hospital record, and that the sample be well-refrigerated (which will retard decomposition) until the analysis has been done.

Expect the police to try to delay your independent test (unless they are very sure that you cannot pass it) by leaving you in the lockup as time dwindles by. Even though most experts will take results of a blood test taken three or more hours after arrest and extrapolate backwards (by figuring the burn-off rate) to calculate the level that existed when you were last operating the automobile, such a method is not desirable. In this instance, make use of the fact that all of your utterances are admissible evidence: Be very insistent that you be allowed immediate access to testing facilities, and direct your request to as many different officers as possible, with those of highest rank being the most important to reach. Be prepared for the fact that if your rights are denied you by the police, a lot of the officers will be prone to lie about what happened to protect the case and their own skins. Don't put all of your evidentiary eggs in a single police basket.

The time to avoid a problem with the cops, when you can, is before it arises. Being forewarned as to what sort of conduct a suspicious police officer is going to be looking for if he stops you, check yourself *before* you turn the ignition switch. Look in the mirror. Is your face flushed? Are your pupils dilated? How do your eyes look generally? Try the field sobriety tests on yourself. Before you drive. Are you able to perform these in such a way that would cause a cop to have doubts that you had been drinking significant amounts of alcohol recently? Unless you can demonstrate these exercises to your own satisfaction, it is unlikely that you will pass muster with a suspicious cop. If in doubt, stay where you are until your condition improves, take a cab, or ride with a friend.

And should you be the host of a gathering where the imbibing has been more than moderate, keep a sharp eye on your guests if you know that they are going to drive themselves home. While they certainly will be punished criminally and sued in civil court if they kill or injure anyone with their automobile, *you* could be sued, too, for letting them get loose when intoxicated, knowing that they intended to drive. At least one state that I know of adopted such a rule a few years ago, and others will follow, inevitably, as civil liability continues to expand.

Which state?

Why, California, of course!

Epilogue

The Drama of Law Enforcement

THE aftermath of the trial was not pleasant. The San Francisco news media howled like small children in their frustration over my acquittal. A police psychologist reported that the cops were "demoralized" by the event, and there was speculation that there might be less zealous police surveillance of drunk drivers as a result. To my face people said, "Good show, glad you beat those bastards," and behind my back they said, "The sonofabitch had so much horsepower he beat the rap!" The fact that I was lucky enough to be able to produce solid *evidence* of my sobriety was quickly lost in the shuffle of public chatter about the event.

I believe San Francisco to be one of the finest cities in America, but, with all due respect, there ought to be some soul-searching going on there. I was arrested by a police officer who, according to the evidence, was given to drinking on duty. The only effort the prosecution made to contradict Ira Jacobowitz involved the testimony of the owner of the Iron Horse who said that Peter Canaan in fact *did* drink on duty, but that it was his, the owner's, understanding that Peter had quit doing that when he was assigned from cruisers to motorcycles. He said Peter didn't want to hurt himself, and expected to be "closer to people" who might smell the booze on his breath.

59

In early 1981, prosecutor Larry Murray was arrested for operating a motor vehicle under the influence and for assault and battery of a police officer. That incident was both ghastly and hilarious, according to police records published during my trial. While a couple of cops were in front of what they thought was an abandoned car, getting ready to raise its front end for towing, they spotted a male figure apparently passed out on the floor of the passenger side of the vehicle. When aroused, Murray announced that he was all right, and turned the ignition key. The car, which was in gear, jumped forward, striking the two police officers, who arrested him for assault and battery on a police officer, and operating under the influence. Murray, who throughout my trial harped on the fact that I thought I was "someone special," reportedly told the officers who arrested him, "You can't treat me like this, I'm an Assistant District Attorney!" And there is more.

According to reports widely circulated in the San Francisco news media, on Tuesday, July 13, 1982, the district attorney, Arlo Smith, and first assistant district attorney, Donald Jacobson—the same gentlemen who decided that a judge of their own court ought not to be entrusted to hear my case without a jury, which would have saved both sides a lot of time and money—were taken by police officers to the Central Police Station at 7:30 P.M. after a complaint had been received of drunken and boisterous conduct. The two men were in their official automobile with the engine running when they were apprehended (which constitutes "operation" in most states, as a matter of law). They were booked and released without a chemical test, after which Jacobson made a public apology for what the news media called a "seven-hour spree." Canaan, Murray, Smith, and Jacobson have not been tried for committing any alcohol-related offenses.

If *you* get picked up at the wheel of a car in San Francisco after a tavern owner has complained that you were objectionably intoxicated, do not expect to be "booked and released." If you are not a

D.A. or a police officer, expect the hammers of hell to descend upon you, whether you are drunk or sober.

I hope the tips in this book will save you and others a lot of grief by giving you clear guidelines as to how much is too much and when you should clearly avoid driving. (If you drive while drunk, I hope you get convicted.) If you get stopped and are not drunk, I hope this book has armed you with advice that will minimize your trouble with cops who sometimes crack down on the innocent and guilty with equal ferocity.

As for Mayor Feinstein of San Francisco, that good lady needs the wisdom of Solomon. She probably doesn't like the idea of chopping down a tree any more than I do, but if Officer Canaan's favorite stop sign is needed for traffic control at that corner, she'd better get the tree in front of it cut down. If she'll assign D.A. Murray to do it personally, I'll come take pictures of the event.

Appendix

Chemical Tests for Intoxication

THIS short description of the chemical tests used to measure alcohol levels in the human body is intended for use by a layman who may be asked to take such a test. It does not purport to be either detailed or scientific. For anyone interested in the subject matter, there are many articles and learned volumes available. I am simply offering a threshhold familiarity to the operators of motor vehicles, and in this effort I am greatly indebted to my long-time friend and associate, John Albert Johnson, who has tried more than five hundred drunken driving cases, lost fewer than a dozen, and —with Bob Shapiro —won mine. I am grateful for his representation then, and his collaboration here.

There are three tests you may be offered, depending on the state in which you are apprehended: urine, blood, and breath. Here are some observations that might serve you well in the future.

Urine

No jurisdiction *requires* a test of the urine, although many offer it. My advice is to avoid it, for several reasons.

First, the accumulation of alcohol in the bladder does not necessarily track the level of alcohol in the blood, and may register substantially higher.

Second, the danger of contamination of the samples from either the hands of the subject or the sample container itself is unacceptably high.

Third, this test requires that two samples be taken, with an interval of at least 20 minutes in between. This is supposed to offset the risk that the bladder specimen level will be higher than the blood level. Those who have been in the business of handling these cases for years are far from convinced that it does.

Blood

This is generally believed to be the most accurate of the chemical tests, and should be the test of choice any time you believe that you are within the legal limits. Unfortunately, police are seldom equipped to administer this test themselves, and will try to talk you into a breath test instead, which *they* can handle.

Basically, through the introduction of chemical reagents into the blood, the alcohol is separated out and measured by volume. The most accurate measurement, however, can be had through the use of gas chromatography, which not all hospitals have available.

The blood test is not without risks. If alcohol is wiped on the skin as an antiseptic before the needle is injected, it may be picked up in the sample and test out to show a level of blood-alcohol which is apparently fatal, or somewhat less than that, which is worse. If, in addition, the blood sample is not tested soon after it is taken, there is a risk that decomposition will occur that can *cause* alcohol to appear which was not present in the system, particularly if the refrigeration of the sample is not very efficient.

There are several ways other than gas chromatography to test blood for alcohol content, all of which, if they are to be accurate, are somewhat complicated and require trained personnel. Insist on being told the qualifications of the person who is to take the sample, as well as those of the person who will test it.

Breath

You may be told that the only test you can take from the police involves a sampling of your breath, and that your refusal to submit will result in the revocation of your license. If you are satisfied that your blood-alcohol level is low and wish to have an end to the matter, you may decide to submit. If you do, make it very plain that you know and can prove that you have had very little to drink, and will require a blood test should the police breath test be adverse to you. The perils in breath tests are substantial.

The basic principle of testing breath samples to determine blood-alcohol level is the notion that twenty-one hundred cubic centimeters of breath (alveolar, or "deep lung" air, as opposed to air from the stomach or "belched" air) equals one cubic centimeter of blood. The various instruments used to test breath are *supposed* to be calibrated to that scale. The operator of this instrument, who may be the arresting officer (although in some states this will be prohibited by law), should be able to satisfy you that he has special training in its use. The brand names of the instruments you might encounter include the following:

> The Gas-Chromatography Intoximeter
> The Intoxilyzer
> The Breathalyzer
> The Intoximeter
> The Drunkometer
> The Alco-Meter

These are listed generally in the order of their reliability, with the Breathalyzer being the most widely used. The last three are seldom seen in police departments today, and if you are offered one of these, be on your guard: someone is way behind the times.

Each of these instruments can give false readings on the high side if residual mouth alcohol—caused by mouthwash, breath sprays, and belching up stomach air—is present at the time of the test.

The Breathalyzer, which you are more likely to encounter than any of the other instruments, uses a sealed ampule of chemicals (potassium dichromate and sulfuric acid) that must be in balance to each other in it if valid results are to be obtained. If they are not, which only a detailed chemical analysis can show, a false high or low reading will result. This instrument also utilizes a photoelectric cell that is supposed to detect a change in color in the breath sample when it is exposed to the ampule. If the photoelectric cell has deteriorated, it will cause false readings on either the high or low side.

The Breathalyzer also contains a valve assembly designed to control the amount of breath that is introduced into the testing chamber. Should this assembly malfunction, erroneous readings on the high side will be caused; in addition, should one of the chemicals in the ampule not remain in solution and concentrate in one end of it or the other, false readings will result. This instrument contains a "null" meter and clutch assembly; any malfunction of these will contaminate both the initial calibration and the reading in a specific test.

To compound matters, there are at least 12 steps which the operator must take, and these vary from model to model, in order to perform a valid test. A mistake in the performance of any of these can invalidate the results; for instance, if the subject is allowed to blow a *second* time into the instrument without the chamber being flushed, an erroneously high reading will occur.

The Intoxilyzer is a far better instrument for the protection of the subject being tested. It is gradually (but much too slowly) replacing the Breathalyzer in police departments around the country, and differs from it in important respects. The Intoxilyzer offers a digital readout that is more accurate than the Breathalyzer's needle indicator. It uses an infrared source of light to detect the alcohol in the sample, rather than the ampule and ultraviolet source used in the Breathalyzer. Should the infrared source of the Intoxilyzer deteriorate, however, its accuracy will also.

The Gas-Chromatography Intoximeter is the most accurate, but takes a highly trained and skilled operator to make it perform. It is in use almost nowhere. Submit to this one only if a trained chemist or toxicologist is conducting the test.

Any of these instruments can be fooled by an abnormal body temperature; if you have a fever, explain to the requesting officer that you *must* have a blood-alcohol test. Finally, the breath tests are subject to manipulation by unscrupulous operators, and the police operators who have to work in the department day after day can hardly be considered to be neutrals if the arresting officer has anything at stake. If you have no alcohol in your system and the police test shows it, the arresting officer may be subject to a lawsuit, a fact of which most of them are aware. If you have had any kind of *disagreement* with the arresting officer, be wary: You will have increased the pressure on the operator of the instrument to avoid demonstrating your innocence with a favorable result.

The whole business of chemical testing for alcohol in the system is, in my judgment, in a most unsatisfactory state. There are simply too many risks imposed on the innocent motorist. It would be a big step forward if only the most accurate equipment were used, and if the testing authority were not the police but an arm of the court with a sworn duty to absolute professionalism and impartiality. The innocent would thus be protected, and the guilty identified in a way that would give courts and juries more confidence in the validity of test results. Convicting drunk drivers is a desirable end. Harassing the innocent is not a necessary part of the process.

Table of State Drunk Driving Laws*

1. *Preliminary Breath Test (PBT):* These tests are for screening purposes and are administered at the site of a traffic stop where the police officer suspects that the driver is operating his or her automobile under the influence of alcohol. The chart indicates the statutory authority for a PBT as well. Moreover, the comments attempt to provide insight into any pecular limitations on PBT's, whether the tests are optional and any penalty for refusal to take a PBT upon a police officer's request.

2. *Blood Alcohol Concentration (BAC) Statutes.* Every state, as well as the District of Columbia, Puerto Rico and the Virgin Islands, presently have statutes governing chemical tests to determine blood alcohol content. The state's right to perform such a test arises from the legal concept of "implied consent." Most state statutes rely on some variation of the Uniform Vehicle Code Section 6-205.1, which, in summary form provides as follows:

---

*The information contained in this table comes primarily from the following report drafted in 1981: *Alcohol Highway Safety Laws: A National Overview,* Compiled by National Traffic Highway Safety Administration, Office of Alcohol Countermeasures, U.S. Dept. of Transportation.

a. The operation of a motor vehicle on a public high-way is deemed to provide a driver's consent to a chemical test of blood, breath or urine to determine BAC.

b. Implied consent usually applies only when driver is arrested for operating or controlling a motor vehicle while under the influence of alcohol.

c. Tests administered by, or under the direction of, a law enforcement officer with reasonable grounds to believe the driver is under the influence.

d. Tests are not administered if the driver refuses, but a refusal results in the revocation of the driver's license.

e. The driver has an opportunity for a hearing to determine if the police officer had probable cause, if there was an arrest and if the driver refused the chemical test.

The chart, in addition to citing the statutory authority for BAC tests, also indicates which states have loosened the requirement of a valid arrest prior to the administering of such test. In addition, any restriction on the type of test is noted. It should be noted that there exists a substantial variation among state statutes concerning the requirement of BAC tests following traffic accidents, but their information has not been included on the chart.

3. *Police Authority:* Most states require licensed medical personnel to perform tests involving the withdrawal of blood. Police officers are usually authorized to conduct breath tests and, to a lesser degree, urine tests. As apparent from the chart, the scope of police authority is often ambiguous.

4. *Defendant's Options:* This category of the chart indicates primarily whether a defendant (the arrested driver) has a choice of the BAC test to be administered and whether there is a right to a supplemental test. Unless otherwise stated, it should be presumed that the supplemental test is to be at the defendant's own expense.

5. *Use of BAC Levels as Evidence in Court:* This category describes the manner in which BAC tests may be used in court.

Each jurisdiction provides that an alcohol/blood ratio of 0.10 percent or more creates at least a presumption, that the defendant can seek to overcome with contrary evidence, that the defendant was under the influence of alcohol (a few states use even lower BAC levels to create a presumption or to be admissible as evidence of intoxication). Where "*per se* illegal" is noted, it means that the 0.10 percent BAC level is conclusive proof of intoxication. California, for instance, has established a distinct crime from the DUI offense (under which 0.10 percent BAC level is considered to raise a presumption), the offense of driving with more than 0.10 blood alcohol concentration (Cal. Veh. Code §23152B), which clearly makes that BAC level *per se* illegal.

6. *Judicial Remedies:* This section describes the penalties and sentences that are required or may be imposed upon first and subsequent convictions. Because some states have rather complex sentencing provisions, this chart only seeks to indicate maximum mandatory and mandatory minimum (where there exists a range of mandatory sentences) terms of imprisonments, and license suspension and revocation requirements. Nearly all states also prescribe fines, but only the existence of mandatory fines has been indicated. In addition, maximum and mandatory license suspensions or revocations are noted. It is important to remember that, except California, this data is compiled from information current through October 31, 1981. While some effort has been made to update the information, because of the increasing national concern over and attention to drunk driving, there have been numerous changes, primarily in the direction of mandatory sentences, to many state DUI statutes and several are under consideration at the time of this writing.

S T A T E	Preliminary Breath Test (PBT) Law[1] Statutory Authority and Comment	Blood Alcohol Concentration (BAC)[2] Statutes and Comment	Police Authority[3]	Defendant's Options[4]	Use of BAC levels as Evidence in Court[5]	Judicial Remedies[6]
Alabama		Ala. Code §32-5-192	Police officer can take both urine & breath specimens. Must afford privacy for urine test.	Can only object to blood test. No right to counsel. Supplemental test permitted at defendant's expense.	Appears .10% BAC illegal per se.	Maximum 1 yr. sentence. Possible 6 mos. license suspension on first offense. Mandatory 6 mos. revocation on second.
Alaska		Alaska Stat. Ann. §28.35.031	Breath testing possible under direction of a police officer.	Police designate test. Supplemental independent test permitted but need not be advised of right to such test.	.10% illegal per se.	Mandatory minimum of 3 day sentence for first offense. Mandatory minimum of 10 days imprisonment for second or subsequent offense if within 5 yrs. of first offense.
Arizona		Ariz. Rev. Stat. Ann. §28-691	Police may take breath sample but expressly may not take urine sample.	Police designate test. Supplemental test permitted.	.10% creates a rebuttable presumption that driver was under the influence.	Mandatory minimum of a 4 day's sentence for first offense, 120 days for subsequent offenses. Mandatory suspension and revocation provisions on first and subsequent convictions.
Arkansas		Ark. Stat. Ann. §75-1045	Police can collect both urine & breath samples.	Police designate test. Defendant must be advised of his right to supplemental test but pay for test himself.	Presumption at .10% BAC.	Mandatory 1 day sentence on first conviction. Up to 1 yr. imprisonment on second and subsequent convictions.

State	Statute	Test Administration	Test Choice	Presumption	Penalties
California	Cal. Vehicle Code §13353 Refusal to take tests results in license suspension for 6 mos. Statute expressly states that driver has no right to consult with an attorney.	Testing of both urine & breath under direction of police. Police do conduct breath test & collect samples.	Defendant has choice of test but there is no sanction if police do not inform of choice. Defendant has right, at his own expense, to supplemental test.	Presumption at .10% BAC under section 23152(a). .10% illegal per se under 23152(b) which proscribes driving with more than .10% blood alcohol.	First offense: Mandatory 3 yrs. informal probation (2 days in jail or 90 day license restriction and attendance at alcohol awareness program) plus mandatory minimum fine, or, if refuse probation, mandatory sentence of 4 days to 6 mos. imprisonment and fine. Second offense: Probation plus mandatory 10 days to 1 yr. imprisonment, fine and license restriction.
Colorado	Colo. Rev. Stat. Ann. §42-4-1202 (3) Consent implied for urine and breath analyses even where no arrest is made provided probable cause to arrest exists and there is a necessity of immediate testing.	Testing of both urine & breath under direction of police.	Defendant may choose blood test but if he doesn't, other tests choice of police. Defendant may have supplemental test.	Presumption at .10% BAC.	Mandatory minimum fines and sentence of 5 days of imprisonment (or 48 hrs. work program). Subsequent convictions yield mandatory minimum 90 day sentence (or 60 hrs. W.P.). First conviction results in automatic 1 yr. maximum license suspension. Subsequent offenses result in minimum five year revocation.

S T A T E	Preliminary Breath Test (PBT) Law[1] Statutory Authority and Comment	Blood Alcohol Concentration (BAC)[2] Statutes and Comment	Police Authority[3]	Defendant's Options[4]	Use of BAC levels as Evidence in Court[5]	Judicial Remedies[6]
Connecticut		Conn. Gen. Stat. Ann. §14-227	Certified person including police officer authorized to take both urine & breath samples.	Defendant chooses tests may have supplemental test.	.10% BAC *prima facie* evidence driver was under influence. .10% illegal *per se* for second or subsequent offenses.	First conviction—6 mos. maximum sentence. Subsequent convictions result in mandatory minimum 6 mos. sentence (waiver possible if enter treatment program). Minimum suspension of 1 yr. after first conviction. Subsequent convictions may result in a minimum 5 yr. sentence.
Delaware		Del. Code Ann. Tit. 21 S2740	Police officer can take both urine & breath samples but only qualified person can conduct urine test.	Police designate test. Defendant may introduce evidence to show inadequacy of test.	.10% BAC illegal per se and samples can be taken as much as 4 hours after alleged offense.	Maximum 6 mos. sentence on first conviction. Maximum 18 mos. sentence on subsequent convictions. Mandatory revocation of license for 1 yr. upon conviction.

Florida	Fla. Stat. Ann. §322.261 Test on driver's demand or with driver's consent. Not admissible in any proceeding.	Fla. Stat. Ann. §322.261 Any detention, based on probable cause, is sufficient lawful arrest to satisfy requirement for implied consent.	Police authorized to take breath samples.	Defendant may request test if police officer has not done so. Supplemental test at defendant's expense authorized.	.10% illegal *per se* or at least *prima facie* evidence of impairment.	Maximum 90 day sentence for first conviction and mandatory 50 hrs. work program. Maximum 1 yr. sentence for subsequent convictions. Mandatory license revocation provisions: maximum 1 yr. for first conviction; minimum 10 yrs. for subsequent convictions.
Georgia	Ga. Code Ann. §688-306		Certified person, including police officer can conduct both urine & breath tests.	Police designate test. Police must advise of right to independent test.	Presumption at .10% BAC.	Maximum 1 yr. sentence but mandatory minimum of 90 days imprisonment for subsequent convictions. Mandatory 1 yr. suspension for first conviction and 5 yr. revocation for subsequent convictions.
Hawaii	Hawaii Rev. Stat. §286-151		Police can take breath sample if collected within 3 hours of alleged DUI violation.	Defendant has the option of which test to take and right to supplemental test.	Presumption at .10% BAC.	1 yr. maximum sentence. If driver accumulates 12 points subsequent convictions will result in mandatory 1 yr. suspension.

S T A T E	Preliminary Breath Test (PBT) Law[1] Statutory Authority and Comment	Blood Alcohol Concentration (BAC)[2] Statutes and Comment	Police Authority[3]	Defendant's Options[4]	Use of BAC levels as Evidence in Court[5]	Judicial Remedies[6]
Idaho		Idaho Code Ann. §49-352	Police officers can probably take both urine & breath specimens.	Not clear who selects test but defendant does have right to supplemental test.	Presumption at .10% BAC.	Maximum 6 mos. sentence for first conviction and 5 yr. maximum for second conviction. Mandatory 90 day suspension for first conviction and 1 yr. for subsequent offenses.
Illinois		Ill. Ann. Stat. ch. 95½, §11-501.1	Certified person including police officer can take both urine & breath samples and direct tests.	Police designate test. Defendant permitted additional test.	Both presumption and illegal per se at .10%.	1 yr. maximum sentence. Minimum revocation of license for 1 yr. and 5 yrs. for first and subsequent convictions, respectively.
Indiana	Ind. Stat. Ann. §9-4-4: Permits some chemical test prior to arrest.	Ind. Stat. Ann. §9-4-4: Driving alone implies consent to BAC test.	Police officer can be among certified persons taking samples.	Appears police designate test. Unclear whether defendant permitted supplemental test.	Presumption at .10% BAC. Evidence of .05% to .10% BAC deemed relevant.	1 yr. maximum sentence for first conviction. 5 days mandatory minimum sentence for subsequent offenses. Mandatory suspensions: 90 days first offense; 1 yr. subsequent convictions.

State	Statute				
Iowa	Iowa Code Ann. §32.B.3	Police can take both urine & breath samples but appears testing to be done by others.	Police designate test but defendant can refuse blood test and independent test permitted.	Presumption at .10%. .137% deemed illegal per se.	48 hrs. mandatory minimum sentence. 5 yrs. maximum sentence for subsequent offenses. Mandatory revocation for first and subsequent convictions.
Kansas	Kan. Stat. Ann. §8-1001	Breath tests conducted under direction of police officer.	Unclear who chooses test. Defendant has right to independent test.	Presumption at .10% BAC.	Mandatory minimum fines plus 1 yr. maximum sentence for first conviction and 90 day mandatory minimum for subsequent offenses. Mandatory 1 yr. suspension for first offense and mandatory minimum 1 yr. revocation for subsequent offenses.
Kentucky	Ky. Rev. Stat. Ann. §186.565	Both breath & urine tests can be conducted under direction of police officer.	Police select test. Defendant may have additional test.	Presumption at .10% BAC.	Maximum 6 mos. sentence for second and subsequent offenses. Mandatory revocation of 6 mos. for first offense and 2 yrs. minimum for subsequent offenses. May be able to avoid initial revocation by attending school.

STATE	Preliminary Breath Test (PBT) Law[1] Statutory Authority and Comment	Blood Alcohol Concentration (BAC)[2] Statutes and Comment	Police Authority[3]	Defendant's Options[4]	Use of BAC levels as Evidence in Court[5]	Judicial Remedies[6]
Louisiana		La. Rev. Stat. Ann. †32:661(A)	Breath & urine samples taken by certified person including police officer but tests done only at direction of police.	Police designate test. Defendant has right to supplemental test.	Presumption at .10% BAC.	Maximum 6 mos. sentence for first conviction. Mandatory minimum of 125 days for second or subsequent convictions. Mandatory suspension for 60 days for first offense & revocation for 1 yr. for subsequent offenses.
Maine	Me. Rev. Stat. Ann. tit. 29 §1312: Police may require PBT; if positive results or if refused, may require chemical tests, refusal of which results in license suspensions."	Me. Rev. Stat. Ann. Tit. 29 §1312: Consent deemed to be given if there is probable cause to believe driver operated or attempted to operate vehicle while under the influence. Before test given driver must be arrested or summoned.	Police can collect breath specimens.	Defendant selects test. Defendant may have right to introduce evidence of supplemental test.	.10% prima facie evidence for some offenses and per se illegal for others.	Mandatory minimum fines plus imprisonment of 2 days minimum for first offense and 60 days for subsequent convictions. Mandatory 45-180 day suspension for first conviction and 90 days-1 yr. suspension for subsequent offenses.
Maryland	Md. Transp. Code Ann. §16-205: No license suspension for refusal. Only defendant may admit results in court.	Md. Transp. Code Ann. §16-205 as amended by Ch. 244 (Laws 1981): Implied consent applies even if person detained on suspicion of driving while under the influ-	Certified person, including a police officer, authorized to take breath sample.	Defendant selects test. Supplemental tests permitted at defendant's own expense.	.08% prima facie evidence of DUI. .13% prima facie evidence of intoxication.	Maximum 1 yr. sentence for first conviction and 2 yrs. for subsequent convictions. 6 mos. minimum revocation for first offense and 18 mos. minimum for subse-

State	Statute			
Massachusetts	Mass. Gen. Laws Ann. ch. 373, off.9/1/82.	Police can take breath sample but consent necessary where seek to get test results by police admissible in evidence.	No express right for defendant to select test but does have right to supplemental test at his own expense.	Presumption at .10%.	Mandatory 1 year loss of license for first conviction of operating under the influence or 30 day suspension if permitted to enter alcohol education program, and maximum 2 year sentence, as well as mandatory minimum fine. Conviction for second offense results in loss of license for 2 years and mandatory minimum sentence of 7 days imprisonment. Mandatory minimum sentence of 60 days for third offense as well as 5 year loss of license.
Michigan	Mich. Stat. Ann. §9.2325(3)	At the request of a police officer, both urine & breath tests can be conducted.	Defendant may demand only a breath test but otherwise choice of test belongs to police. Defendant has right to additional test.	Presumption of under the influence at .10% BAC. Excess of .07% but less than .10% raises presumption of impairment.	90 day maximum sentence and 2 yr. maximum license suspension for first offense. Maximum 5 yr. sentence and 2 yr. suspension for subsequent convictions. Mandatory sentence for third offense.

S T A T E	Preliminary Breath Test (PBT) Law[1] Statutory Authority and Comment	Blood Alcohol Concentration (BAC)[2] Statutes and Comment	Police Authority[3]	Defendant's Options[4]	Use of BAC levels as Evidence in Court[5]	Judicial Remedies[6]
Minnesota	Minn. Stat. Ann. §169.121, as amended by Laws 1982 c. 423. Only used as guide for police officer's decision to arrest or require BAC tests. No suspension for refusal.[b]	Minn. Stat. Ann. §169.123(2): Consent implied also when driver involved in accidents, when PBT refused or when PBT shows BAC of .10% or more.	Testing under direction of police officer possible. Police may be able to take samples.	Defendant may decline blood test and select either breath or urine test. Independent test at defendant's expense permitted.	.10% illegal per se.	Maximum sentence of 90 days imprisonment and $500 fine for first offense; for second conviction within 5 years, maximum 1-year sentence and $1000 fine. Mandatory minimum 30-day revocation for first offense; 90-day mandatory minimum revocation for second conviction within 5 years and 1 year for third conviction within 5 years.
Mississippi	Miss. Code Ann. §63-11-5: Unofficial test before chemical test. Need arrest for official test.	Miss. Code Ann. §63-11-5	Police can take samples for urine & breath & tests can be conducted at their direction.	Appears police designate test. At his own expense, defendant may have independent test.	Presumption at .10% BAC.	Mandatory fine on first conviction, maximum sentence of 1 yr. for subsequent convictions. Mandatory suspensions of 1 yr. for first conviction and 2 yrs. for subsequent convictions.
Missouri		Mo. Rev. Stat. §577.020(1)	Appears certified persons including police can take urine samples & police can conduct breath tests.	Unclear who designates test. Right to supplemental test exists.	.10% prima facie evidence of intoxication but appears to be illegal per se for driving offense.	Maximum 6 mos. sentence for first conviction. 10 yrs. for subsequent offenses. Based on point system, mandatory 30 day suspension for first conviction, 1 yr. revocation for subsequent offenses.

Montana	Mont. Code Ann. §61-8-402(1): Arrest is not necessary if driver is unconscious or in a condition which disables him from refusal according to court decisions.	Police can request urine & breath samples.	Police select tests. Defendant permitted supplemental test.	Presumption at .10% BAC.	Maximum 24 hrs. sentence for first offense, maximum 1 yr. sentence for subsequent offenses with certain provisions for mandatory sentence upon third offense. Mandatory 6 mos. suspension for first offense, 1 yr. revocation for subsequent convictions.
Nebraska	Neb. Rev. Stat. §39-669.08: Refusal to submit or finding of .10% alcohol content grounds for arrest. No suspension for refusal.	Neb. Rev. Stat. §39-669.08	Other than PBT, person needs a permit to conduct breath & urine tests.	Defendant may select between blood and urine tests if they are designated by police. Supplemental test permitted.	.10% illegal *per se*.	Mandatory fines and sentences, 7 day maximum for first offense, 6 mos. for subsequent offenses. Mandatory suspension and revocation provisions for first and subsequent convictions.
Nevada	Nev. Rev. Stat. §484.383(1)	Urine & breath testing possible under police direction.	Under most circumstances defendant has choice. He is also authorized to have supplemental test.	Presumption at .10% BAC.	Maximum 6 mos. sentence for first offense. Mandatory permanent revocation of license for second or subsequent offenses.

S T A T E	Preliminary Breath Test (PBT) Law[1] Statutory Authority and Comment	Blood Alcohol Concentration (BAC)[2] Statutes and Comment	Police Authority[3]	Defendant's Options[4]	Use of BAC levels as Evidence in Court[5]	Judicial Remedies[6]
New Hampshire		N.H. Rev. Stat. Ann. §265:84	Same as Nevada.	Police designate test but must inform defendant of right to independent test.	.10% *prima facie* evidence of intoxication.	Mandatory minimum 7 day sentence for second or subsequent offense within 7 yr. period. First offense yields mandatory 60 days to 2 yrs. revocation of license. 3 yrs. for subsequent convictions.
New Jersey		N.J. Stat. Ann. §39:4-502 Test need not be incidental to lawful arrest but probable cause for arrest must exist. Driver cannot refuse breathalyzer and anyone who refuses chemical test will have license suspended or revoked.	Same as Nevada but certified persons including police can take both urine & breath samples.	Police may designate breath test. Other tests choice of defendant after advised of right by police.	Presumption at .10% BAC.	Maximum 30 day sentence for first conviction. Mandatory imprisonment and fine for subsequent offenses. Mandatory suspension for first offense and revocation for subsequent offenses.
New Mexico		N.M. Stat. Ann. §§6-8-10, 66-8-105 to 66-8-112: Must have lawful arrest prior to test or actual consent, otherwise results inadmissible in court.	Breath testing is possible under direction of a police officer.	Unclear who selects test but defendant has choice of supplemental test at State's expense.	Presumption at .10% BAC.	Maximum 90 days sentence for first offense, 1 yr. for subsequent offenses. Mandatory 1 yr. revocation unless complete a driver rehabilitation program.

New York	N.Y. Veh. & Traf. Law §1193a: Drivers in accidents given PBT to determine need for BAC tests.	N.Y. Veh. Traf. Law §1194 §1193(a): If involved in an accident or violate rules of the road may be required to take a breath test. Results used to determine need for further tests and no penalty for refusal to take test.	Same as New Jersey	Appears police designate initial test while defendant has choice of supplemental test.	More than .07% but less than .10% *prima facie* evidence of impairment. .10% illegal per se.	1 yr. maximum sentence for first offense. 4 yrs. maximum for subsequent offenses. Revocation of license for minimum of 6 mos. for first and subsequent convictions.
North Carolina	N.C. Gen. Stat. §20-16: Driver need not submit to PBT nor is test result admissible in court	N.C. Gen. Stat. §20-16	Same as New Mexico. Police expressly prohibited from administering tests.	Police designate test. Defendant has right to additional test.	.10% per se illegal.	First offense, 6 mos. maximum sentence and mandatory 1 yr. license revocation. Subsequent offenses: mandatory fine, 3 days of imprisonment (at minimum) and permanent revocation.
North Dakota	N.D. Cent. Code §39-20: Revocation or suspension of license for refusal to submit to PBT. Results used to determine whether BAC test necessary.	N.D. Cent. Code §39-20	Unclear whether police may administer tests for urine & breath, but they may request same.	Police designate test and appear to have right to supplemental test.	Presumption at .10% BAC.	No mandatory sentence for first offense but 3 day minimum 1 yr. maximum sentence for subsequent offenses. Mandatory suspension based on point system.
Ohio	Ohio Rev. Code Ann. §4511-191 (A)		Same as New Jersey.	Police designate test. Supplemental test permitted.	Presumption at .10% BAC.	First offense: mandatory minimum 3 day sentence and 30 days—3 yrs. suspension of license. Same for subsequent offenses.

S T A T E	Preliminary Breath Test (PBT) Law[1] Statutory Authority and Comment	Blood Alcohol Concentration (BAC)[2] Statutes and Comment	Police Authority[3]	Defendant's Options[4]	Use of BAC levels as Evidence in Court[5]	Judicial Remedies[6]
Okla-homa		Okla. Stat. Ann. titl. 47, §751	Police can direct that breath test be taken & may be able to take sample.	Defendant selects test and may have additional test.	Presumption at .10% BAC.	Mandatory fines and 10 day mandatory minimum sentence for first offense, 1 yr. for subsequent convictions. Mandatory maximum 1 yr. license revocation.
Oregon		Ore. Rev. Stat. §487.805.487.835: Implied consent only for chemical test of breath. Other chemical tests require express consent (voluntary, informed and with opportunity to seek advice of counsel).	Testing of both urine & breath possible under direction of police.	Defendant can choose between breathalyzer and have supplemental test at own expense.	.10% per se illegal.	1 yr. maximum sentence. Mandatory 1 yr. suspension for first offense.
Penn-sylvania		Pa. Stat. Ann. ch. 75, §1547: Implied consent for breath, blood tests if reasonable grounds to believe a person driving under the influence exists. Refusal to take test results in license suspension.	A certified person including a police officer authorized to take breath sample.	Police choose test. Defendant may have additional test but need not be informed of right to test.	Presumption at .10% BAC.	Maximum 1 yr. sentence. Mandatory 6 mos. license suspension for first conviction and mandatory revocation for subsequent offenses.

State	Statute				
Rhode Island	R.I. Gen. Laws Ann. §31-27-2.1	Same as New Jersey.	Unclear who designates test but supplemental test results admissible.	Presumption at .10% BAC.	Mandatory work program for first offense and mandatory minimum 6 mos. sentence for subsequent offenses. Mandatory minimum 3 mos. suspension for first offense and 2 yr. suspension for subsequent offenses.
South Carolina	S.C. Code Ann. §56-5-2950	Police may not take breath sample but may request breath test.	Police may designate breath test. Defendant may have supplemental test.	Presumption at .10% BAC.	Maximum 30 day sentence for first conviction and 3 yr. sentence for subsequent offenses. Mandatory 6 mos. suspension of license for first offense which increases for subsequent convictions.
South Dakota	S.D. Code §32-23; S.D. Code §32-23: Used to determine whether further testing is necessary.	Testing possible under the direction of a police officer for both urine & breath.	Police designate test. At his own expense, defendant may have supplemental test.	Presumption at .10%. Above .10% *per se* illegal.	Maximum 1 yr. sentence for first conviction and 2 yrs. for subsequent convictions. Mandatory minimum revocation for 30 days and 1 yr. for subsequent convictions.

STATE	Preliminary Breath Test (PBT) Law[1] Statutory Authority and Comment	Blood Alcohol Concentration (BAC)[2] Statutes and Comment	Police Authority[3]	Defendant's Options[4]	Use of BAC levels as Evidence in Court[5]	Judicial Remedies[6]
Tennessee		Tenn. Code Ann. §55-10-406: Police officer need only have reasonable ground to believe driver under influence to imply consent. However, arrest is prerequisite to imposing penalty for refusal to submit to test.	Same as South Dakota.	Unclear who has choice of test. Police need not advise of right of supplemental test.	Presumption at .10% BAC.	Mandatory minimum fines and 48 hours of imprisonment for first offense, 120 days for subsequent offenses. Mandatory revocation of license provisions for first and subsequent convictions.
Texas		Tex. Rev. Civ. Stat. Ann. 6701 1-5(1). Implied consent only for chemical test of breath. Other BAC tests need express consent.	Certified police officers can take breath sample & police can request test.	Defendant selects test. Supplemental tests must be conducted within 2 hours of arrest.	Presumption at .10% BAC.	Mandatory minimum 3 day sentence for first offense, 10 days for subsequent offenses. Mandatory 12 mos. suspension for first offense, 18 mos. for subsequent convictions.
Utah		Utah Code Ann. §41-6-44.10(a): Police officer need only have grounds to believe that person driving under the influence. Arrest necessary requirement to impose penalty for refusal to submit to test.	Breath & urine tests can be conducted under direction of police officer.	Police specify test. At defendant's expense he is permitted supplemental test.	Presumption at .08% BAC. .10% per se illegal.	Mandatory minimum 2 days imprisonment for first offense (or 2 days work program), 30 days for subsequent offenses.

Vermont	Vt. Stat. Ann. tit. 23 §120(b): Test administered one or more times to determine need for BAC test but result inadmissible.	Vt. Stat. Ann. tit. 23 §1202(b): Arrest apparently not a prerequisite for implied consent.	Police officer can collect breath specimen.	Police designate test. Supplemental test permitted.	.10% creates both presumption and a per se illegal act.	Maximum 1 yr. sentence. Mandatory 1 yr. suspension of license for first conviction.
Virginia	Va. Code Ann. §18.2-267(a): Results of PBT inadmissible in court.	Va. Code Ann. §18.2-268(b).	A certified police officer can take breath sample but arresting officer cannot conduct tests.	Defendant selects test and may have blood from supplemental test sent to lab of his choice.	Presumption at .10% BAC.	Maximum 12 mos. sentence for first offense coupled with mandatory license suspension. Mandatory minimum fine and 2 mos. imprisonment for subsequent offenses and minimum 3 yr. license revocation.
Washington	Wash. Rev. Code Ann. §46.20.308(1): Unless person unconscious, only a breath test allowed. Blood tests without consent if driver arrested for negligent homicide or DUI following serious accident.		Testing possible for breath under direction of police officer.	Police in most circumstances may designate breath test. Limited right to supplemental test.	Same as Vermont.	Mandatory fines, mandatory minimum 1 day in jail for first offense, 7 days for subsequent offenses. Mandatory minimum 30 day suspension for first offense. Mandatory revocation for third conviction.
West Virginia	W. Va. Code Ann. §17C-5: PBT results only used to determine whether BAC test necessary.	W. Va. Code Ann. §17C-5: Anyone arrested for driving while intoxicated may demand a BAC test.	Police may take both urine & breath samples & test may be conducted under their direction.	Police designate test. Supplemental test at defendant's own expense.	.10% prima facie evidence of intoxication.	Mandatory minimum 1 day sentence for first offense, 1 yr. for third or subsequent offense. Mandatory revocation of license for third or subsequent offense.

STATE	Preliminary Breath Test (PBT) Law[1] Statutory Authority and Comment	Blood Alcohol Concentration (BAC)[2] Statutes and Comment	Police Authority[3]	Defendant's Options[4]	Use of BAC levels as Evidence in Court[5]	Judicial Remedies[6]
Wisconsin	Wis. Stat. Ann. §343.305. Refusal of request to take PBT made prior to arrest or issuance of citation, may be done without penalty if driver agrees to BAC test.[d]	Wis. Stat. Ann. §343.305	Same as West Virginia.	Police designate test. Supplemental test permitted.	.10% per se illegal.	Mandatory minimum fines and 30 day sentence for third or subsequent conviction. Mandatory suspension for 3-6 mos. for first conviction. For subsequent offenses—revocation.
Wyoming		Wyo. Stat. Ann. §31-6-102(a)	Testing is possible for breath & urine under police direction.	Defendant has choice of tests at his expense and right to supplemental tests.	Presumption at .10% BAC.	Maximum 6 mos. sentence for first conviction, mandatory minimum 7 days for subsequent offenses. Mandatory 3 mos. suspension for first offense, 6 mos. for second.
District of Columbia		D.C. Code Ann. 840-502(a) (b)	Police can collect urine & breath samples & tests possible under police officer's direction.	Defendant chooses test unless unreasonable delay will result. Has right to supplemental test.	.10% BAC is *prima facie* evidence of intoxication.	Mandatory revocation of license for conviction. Imprisonment optional.

Puerto Rico	P.R. Laws Ann. tit. 9 §1043	P.R. Laws Ann. tit. 9 §1043: "Initial breath test" performed in addition to BAC tests to see if chemical test necessary.	Testing is possible for breath under direction of police officer.	Defendant has choice of tests and may have independent analysis of blood.	Presumption at .10% BAC.	Mandatory license suspension until successful completion of driver's improvement program. Possible fine or imprisonment, or both.
Virgin Islands	V.I. Code Ann. tit. 20, §4933(e)		Testing for urine & breath under police direction & they may be able to take specimens.	Appears defendant has no choice of test but may have right to supplemental test of blood.	.10% BAC is *prima facie* evidence of intoxication.	Mandatory minimum 6 mos. suspension for first conviction. No mandatory imprisonment.

a. In addition, results of BAC test are *prima facie* evidence of blood alcohol.

b. PBT results in Minnesota are not admissible in court except to show that subsequent chemical test was properly required.

c. Driving under the influence.

d. PBT results are expressly made inadmissible in court by statute in Wisconsin.